BUDDHISM

AND

CHRISTIANITY

FACE TO FACE;

OR AN ORAL DISCUSSION BETWEEN THE

REV. MIGETTUWATTE,		REV. D. SILVA,
A	} AND {	AN
BUDDHIST PRIEST,		ENGLISH CLERGYMAN.

HELD AT PANTURA, CEYLON.

WITH AN

INTRODUCTION AND ANNOTATIONS

BY

J. M. PEEBLES, M.D.,

Fellow of the Academy of Sciences, New Orleans, U.S.A.;
Fellow of the Anthropological Society, London;
Corresponding Member of the Psychological Society of
Great Britain; Corresponding Member of the
Oriental Society of Archæology, India, &c.

BOSTON:

COLBY AND RICH, PUBLISHERS,

9 MONTGOMERY PLACE.

PREFACE.

WITH an admiration of the calmness that characterises the Oriental mind, and a deep interest in the symbolisms that underlie the Eastern religions, I had long desired to see these religions, especially Buddhism, brought into the arena of discussion face to face with the Christian religion, that each system might be subjected to the test of controversy. This was partially done awhile since at Pantura, Ceylon, where a Buddhist priest met, in an oral debate, the Rev. Mr. Silva, a Wesleyan minister.

The discussion continued two days, before an almost breathless audience, numbering at times from five to seven thousand in attendance. Each of the parties had their sympathising friends, and both, as usual, claimed the victory. So far as I heard expressions from what seemed to be impartial minds, they were to the end that the Buddhist priest, being the most graceful speaker, and adapting himself to the popular mind, carried the multitude with him. It is certain that some of the Christians did not feel satisfied with the result.

The debate was reported, and a few copies published by John Capper, Esq., Editor of the *Ceylon Times*. "The report," so he says, "has been revised by the respective disputants, so that it may be taken as a correct account of what passed. The Pali extracts were revised by Rev. C. Alwis and a portion by Mr. L. de Zoysa, the Government interpreter."

INTRODUCTION.

"A pilgrim through eternity,
  In countless births have I been born."

"Mind is the root; actions proceed from the mind. If any one speak or act from a corrupt mind, suffering will follow, as the dust follows the rolling wheeL"

BUDDHA.

ONLY think of it—there are estimated to be 500,000,000 of Buddhists in Ceylon, China, Japan, Thibet, Burmah, Siam, and other Eastern coun ries—something like one-third of the whole human race!

The founder of this vast body of religionists was Guatama Buddha, born at Kapilavastu, in Northern India, about the year 556 B. C., according to Max Müller, and the best Hindu authority. He belonged by descent to the Sakya clan—the proud Solar race of India. Passing by his earlier years, given to meditation and reverie—passing by the spiritual marvels that preceded his public teachings, it is but the commonest justice to say that he hallowed the nation that gave him birth, and that his practical teachings have become largely the common heritage of humanity.

"On Himalaya's lonely steep
    There lived of old a holy sage,
    Of shrivelled form, and bent with age,
  Inured to meditations deep.

He—when great Buddha had been born,
    The glory of the Sakya race,
    Endowed with every holy grace
  To save the suffering world forlorn—

Behold strange portents, signs which taught
  The wise, that that auspicious time
  Had witnessed some event sublime,
With universal blessings fraught.

*   *   *   *   *

But once, O men, in many years,
  The fir-tree somewhere flowers, perhaps;
  So after countless ages lapse,
A *Buddha* once on earth appears!

The world of men and gods to bless,
  The way of rest and peace to teach,
  A holy law this *god* did preach—
A law of stainless righteousness.

If, spurning worldly pomp as vain,
  You choose to lead a tranquil life,
  And wander forth from home and wife,
You, too, a Buddha's rank shall gain."

Great thinkers, great self-sacrificing souls such as Buddha, are the makers of history, and the standard-bearers of the ages. They live immortal in books, and more so, if possible, in the memories of admiring worshippers.

Guatama Budlha, drinking from the fountain of inspiration, became, long before the Christian era, a central and radiating sun, the light from which crystallised into Buddhism, the *one* great religious institution of the Orient. And now, after a lapse of over 2000 years, it is still afire with energy and spiritual vitality. Its shrines multiply; converts flock to its standard; and thoughtful minds in far-away Europe and America are more and more attracted to its catholic spirit and broad tolerant principles.

The editor of the oldest daily newspaper in the island of Ceylon—the *Ceylon Times*—had a little while since the following editorial touching the status and progress of Buddhism in Ceylon:—

" There is no doubt that whilst we are congratulating ourselves on the successful work of our missionary and educational establishments, the Buddhists are stimulated by the same success to fresh efforts in behalf of their own faith.

Not only have one or two of the most educated men amongst them, priests and laymen, put forward pamphlets and periodicals in the vernacular, in defence and illustration of their creed, but there is a greater activity generally amongst the Buddhist priesthood, with the object of awakening in the minds of the people a more lively fe·ling tow.rds their faith. Religious services are now being held every Sunday, as the appointed day of rest amongst nearly all classes, whereas it was the wont of the priesthood some few years ago to call their congregations together only on the occasion of some day memorable in their calendar for its sanctity. Temples are in course of construction, and where such work is not immediately practicable, temporary structures have been erected in which the people may assemble, and seated on benches listen to the recital of 'Bana,' and the exhortations and illustrations of the ministering priest.

* * * * *

" One such structure of rather large size we entered on a recent Sunday. The service was conducted by Sipkadua Sumangalabhidana, High Priest of Adam's Peak, the most accomplished Pali scholar in the island. He commenced by the recital of 'Bana,' in the responses to which the assembled congregation joined in a most proper and devout manner. At the conclusion of the prayer, the High Priest, always seated, and holding a small talipot fan in his hand, commenced his address, which was intended as an introduction to a course of lectures on Buddhism.

" The learned High Priest commenced enumerating some of the most important Buddhist books, and briefly explaining their contents, and the objects for which they were written. He stated that Buddha's doctrines may be divided into two parts—one the philosophical portion, containing sublime truths which only the eminently learned can understand, and the other, the plain discourses, embodying great truths, but couched in homely language. The homely language used, the priest went on to say, often conveyed false ideas with it, but such language was made the medium of conveying facts, with the view of adapting himself to the capacities of the common people, and he would particularly remind them that they were not to suppose that the ' Great High Buddha ' meant to countenance the superficial meaning which those words implied.

* * * * *

"After speaking of the importance of works, of the necessity of *personal merit*, he enlarged upon *Sowan, Sakradagami, Anagami,* and *Arhat,* the four paths of virtue prescribed by Buddha to obtain *Nirwana* (at the mention of which all the assembled crowd cried *Sadu*); he concluded a learned sermon of some two hours' duration by exhorting the congregation to exercise patience, and to follow Buddha's command of not even so much as *thinking* evil of those who cruelly used and persecuted them.

"The priest had neither book nor any notes to refer to, but the able manner in which he freely quoted from the various Pali works, giving the title of every book in support of his statements, the clear, logical manner in which he reasoned, explaining each difficult term he used, giving even the derivation of each word, and the able summing up, was, to say the least, very remarkable.

"Attached to the temple, which is to be erected on the ground now occupied by the temporary building, will be a college for priests and laymen, in which Pali alone will be taught to such students as may frequent it for secular education only, and the High Priest stated how gladly he would give instruction to any English gentleman desiring to learn the Pali language."

THE DOCTRINES OF BUDDHISM—NIRVANA.

Buddhism has been charged with atheism. This is rank injustice, It is true that Buddhists do not believe in a personal, human-shaped God, the subject of limitations, and even of such passions as anger and jealousy; but they *do* believe in a Supreme Power—the ineffable, the infinite Presence. They further believe that this ever-present God will not in some remote period judge the world, but that he is incarnate in *all* worlds, and in the self-executive laws that pertain to the physical and moral universe. Accordingly, to the enlightened Buddhist, life is a sowing and a reaping—a measureless series of causes and effects—of sins and punishments, until the attainment of *Nirvana.* Then it is *soul-life,* in endless unfoldment.

There has been much useless, if not really idle talk as to what Buddha meant, and what modern Buddhists still mean, by entrance into *Nirvana.* What I have to say upon this matter is not from prejudice; nor is it gathered from the booked sayings and missionary fragments so often referred to in current literature; but rather from inquiries in the homes, the temples, and the colleges of the priests. It seems a little difficult for missionaries to see the bright and beautiful side of what they denominate " heathenism." That it has its excrescences and superstitions I freely admit; and may not the same be said of all the great religions of the world. So far as missionaries teach the people of the East the English language; so far as they instruct them in the arts and sciences, and encourage secular education generally, they do great good; but in matters of religion they have nothing *new* to take the Orientals that is *true*.

I have talked personally with scores of learned Buddhist priests in Ceylon, China, and other Eastern countries; and with a single exception, they assured me that entrance into *Nirvana* was emancipation from pains, sorrows, and disappointments, final release from re-births and a sweet, divine, yet conscious *repose* that no language can fully express. And this one priest who took a different view, did not believe in the soul's absolute annihilation, but rather in its subjective, unconscious existence—something akin to final absorption into the unknowable!

It must be evident to every impartial student of the Oriental religions that the aspirations of Buddhists, the true construction of their ancient writings, and the present testimony of their most learned priests, *all* go to shew that *Nirvana* is not, in even a subordinate sense, extinction of conscious existence! And further, it is most distinctly stated in the Buddhist Scriptures—*scriptures* that may be traced to the age of Guatama Buddha himself—that Buddha enjoyed *Nirvana* while yet in his mortal body; and that he appeared to his disciples in his glorified state after his physical dissolution. To this end Max Müller says: " If we consider that Buddha himself, after he had already seen *Nirvana*, still remains on earth until his body falls a prey to death; that in the legends Buddha appears to his disciples, even after his death; it seems to me that all these circumstances are hardly reconcilable with the orthodox metaphysical doctrine of *Nirvana*." Again, he says: " *Nirvana* means the extinction of many things: of *selfishness, desire*, and *sin* without going so far as the extinction of consciousness, and even existence."

In reviewing Max Müller's "Dhammapada," James D'Alexis, F.R.A.S., and Member of the Parliamentary Council of Ceylon, after admitting that Guatama Buddha attained not only Buddahood, but a foretaste of *Nirvana* while yet in his body, through temperance, self-sacrifice, prayer, and holy living, thus continues: "But the relative happiness of the Buddhist *Nirvana* is one which is acquired in this very life. He who reaches the end of births has attained *Nirvana*. He who has received his last body, and is yet alive, has attained *Nirvana*. These and numerous other texts clearly shew that man attains *Nirvana* in this very life." And so a similar class of texts in the New Testament shew that *Nirvana*—eternal life, that is, spiritual life—is to be attained in a degree and largely enjoyed in this present world. Such is the import of these Biblical passages: "And this *is* life eternal;" "I am the resurrection and the life;" "Walk in the spirit;" "Be of good cheer, I have overcome the world." That religious body known in América as Shakers, and who in doctrines and practices more nearly resemble the Buddhists than any other class of religionists, denominate this *Nirvana-life*, the resurrection-life. It is the calm, serene life of the soul, virtually lifted out of, and living above the plane of the carnal nature and the earthly passions. It is spiritual emancipation and victory!

Buddha, speaking of a Rahan named *Thamula*, said "he had conquered all his passions, and attained the state of Nirvana."

When a Buddhist, through aspiration and effort, has attained a very high degree of spirituality, he is considered a *Rahat*. And these Rahats, by dieting, by fasting, and prayer, become so spiritual, so ethereal that they can rise in the air, control to some degree the elements, and can even become invisible, or vanish from sight, as did Jesus when walking upon earth so many days in. his spiritually-materialised body.

Nagasena, a Buddhist missionary before the Christian era, said : "*Nirvana* is' the divine rest ; the destroying of the infinite sorrow of the world, the abode of abodes that cannot be explained."

And Wong-Chin-Fu, a Chinese scholar and Buddhist, who has been recently travelling in America, remarked repeatedly : "By *Nirvana* we all understand a final re-union with God, coincident with the perfection of the human spirit by its ultimate disembarrassment of matter. It is the very opposite of *personal annihilation*."

In the opinion of all thoughtful Buddhists, *Nirvana* is to be obtained only through struggle, self-denial, renunciation of worldly pleasures, release from selfish entanglements, abstemious living, holy aspiration, and a sweet trust in the illimitable, ineffable Oversoul of the Universe. And it consists in the fruition of all hopes, the realisation of all enchanting dreams, the fulfilment of all divine prophecies, the eternal becoming, the fadeless glory of a conscious immortality !

THE SACRIFICIAL ATONEMENT.

The great system of Buddhism knows nothing of a crucified Saviour—nothing of salvation through atoning blood. Its basic foundation rests upon the immutable principle of cause and effect. Sin and punishment, virtue and happiness are inseparably connected, according to the doctrines of Guatama Buddha. Listen :—

"Sin will come back upon the sinful, like fine dust thrown against the wind."

"An evil deed does not turn suddenly like milk; but smouldering, it follows the fool, like fire covered by ashes."

"Thyself is its own defence, its own refuge ; it atones for its own sins ; none can purify another."

"All we are is the result of what we have thought. If a man speaks or acts with evil thoughts, pain follows, as the wheel the foot of him who draws the carriage."

"The virtuous man rejoices in this world, and he will rejoice in the next ; in both worlds has he joy. He rejoices, he exults, seeing the purity of his deed."

"These wise people, meditative, steady, always possessed of strong powers, attain to Nirvana, the highest felicity !"

In the "Indian Saint; or Buddha and Buddhism," a most excellent volume by C. D. B. Mills, the author declares that "There is no doctrine of commercial substitution here, nor a shade of our Western dream of atonement by vicarious blood." He further says that " Spence Hardy, a Wesleyan missionary, many years resident in Ceylon, finds this one of the most hopeless things in the prospect regarding the conversion of the Buddhists; they know nothing of the salvation by blood; it is so foreign to their entire system of religion that there is found no place in the Oriental mind wherein to graft such a conception. The Buddhist knows nothing of an atonement."

THE MORAL INFLUENCE OF BUDDHISM.

The tone of morality is higher, and the practice of charitable deeds far more prevalent in Buddhist than in Christian countries. . This will be conceded by every unprejudiced traveller, and by every candid and trustworthy foreign resident of Ceylon, Siam, China, and the East. Only last week a bull-fight was indulged in at Madrid, in honour of the marriage festival of the King and Queen. And Spain, remember, is a Christian country. Magnificent cathedrals dot the great cities, and costly churches crown the hill-tops. The cross is the dominant symbol, and Mass is the solemn song, and the ever-recurring echo of the passing years. And yet the nobility—the *élite*, even the ladies, of the realm, assemble to witness a brutal bull-fight; where Christian men, dressed like savages, shake crimson rags at bulls to madden them for the bloody fray! And when these poor animals' sides were pierced with flaming goads; when the hides of the horses were ripped and torn; when the men in the ring were bruised and wounded; and when pools of blood covered the ground, these ladies—the Christian ladies of Roman Catholic Spain—cheered and waved their handkerchiefs—so say the Spanish journals! It is sad to write, though true, that bull-fights, dog-fights, and men-fights—the latter under the name of *war*—indicate the status of Christian morals in this evening-time of the nineteenth century.

The columns of the English newspapers are often crowded with records of drunkenness, robberies, midnight fightings, and high-handed murders. The London *Times*, treating of a terrible murder that transpired a few days ago in the West End, says :—

" The circumstances, as we have them set out palpably before us, are a miserable revelation of the brutality of which men and women living around us are capable."

In America, with its 60,000 clergymen, millions of Bibles, and salaried revivalists, the state of morals is no better. Of this the public journals offer abundant proof. The editor of the *Hornellsville Times* declares that—

" The records of the past have never presented a more fearful and corrupt state of society than now exists *throughout the United States*. The newspapers from every quarter are becoming more and more loaded with the records of crime."

The *Scientific American* says :—

" It is admitted by all parties that crimes of the most outrageous and unprecedented character abound throughout the country to a degree wholly unparalleled."

Though I have travelled twice around the world spending days in Buddhist temples, months in the homes of Brahmans and Buddhists, and years in their countries, I never saw a Buddhist in a state of intoxication. Murder is comparatively unknown; theft is uncommon; and profanity prevails only so far as Oriental people have mingled with the Christian nations of the West. To this end, Wong-Chin-fu a Chinese orator and Buddhist, said, when lecturing in Chicago, U.S.A.—

" I challenge any man to say that he ever heard a Chinese man, woman, or child, take the name of Almighty God in vain, unless it was in the English language after he had become demoralised."

Bishop Bigandet testifies not only to the general kindheartedness, chastity, and morality of Buddhists, but to the ameliorating influences of the system upon woman. Their religion ignores caste, and they naturally accept the theory that we are all brothers. Their hearts seem full of tenderness. They carefully care for the sick and the aged. Reverence and love for parents is proverbial in the East.

The following constitutes the ethical code, or the five great commandments of the Buddhists:—

    I. Thou shalt not kill.

    II. Thou shalt not steal.

    III. Thou shalt not commit adultery.

    IV. Thou shalt not speak untruths.

    V. Thou shalt not take any intoxicating drink.

This moral code has been amplified in some of the Buddhist countries, the commandments being increased to ten in number. Substantially embodying the five, and adding others from their sacred canon, they stand thus:—

    I. Thou shalt kill no animal whatever, from the meanest insect up to man.

    II. Thou shalt not steal.

    III. Thou shalt not violate the wife of another.

    IV. Thou shalt speak no word that is false.

    V. Thou shalt not drink wine, nor anything that may intoxicate.

    VI. Thou shalt avoid all anger, hatred, and bitter language.

    VII. Thou shalt not indulge in idle and vain talk.

    VIII. Thou shalt not covet thy neighbour's goods.

    IX. Thou shalt not harbour envy, nor pride, nor revenge, nor malice, nor the desire of thy neighbour's death or misfortune.

    X. Thou shalt not follow the doctrines of false gods.

Those who keep these commandments; who subdue their passions; who strive to live up to their divinest ideal; who through struggle conquer their selfishness, and hold the perfect mastery over the lower earthly self, are on the way to *Nirvana*—the rest of Buddha.

" The rest of Boodh ! The starry rest of Boodh !
  The lore of old, and the ancestral feud,
  Shall move no more, forgotten and forgiven,
  In the repose of Heaven.
  The stars may fall ; the sun be turned to blood ;
  The earth be shrouded in a fiery flood ;
  The heavens be rolled together as a scroll ;
  The form and face of nature be renewed ;
  Still shall abide the all-pervading Soul,
  And still the *calm* of those who rest in Boodh."

WHAT DO BUDDHISTS EAT?—AND WHAT ARE THEIR AIMS OF LIFE?

The word Buddha signifies enlightened—divinely illumined. Though Guatama Buddha sought to induce others to become self-sacrificing and pure, that *they* might also become Buddhas, he professed no infallible leadership. On the contrary, choosing a peaceful life of self-denial, he hid himself behind the doctrines and truths he uttered. And this has ever been my aim, whether in my native country, or afar in foreign lands. It has also been the noble aim of my co-workers in this reconstructive era of angel ministrants. Inspirational truths, moral conquests, and impersonal principles are the true leaders that lead men up on to the mountain tops of holiness and harmony. The truths enunciated by that great Indian sage, Buddha, have led millions in the way of the better life.

Rice is the great staple of food in all Buddhist countries; and the general teachings of Buddhist priests are in favour of vegetables, grains, and fruits, as food. Though some of these religionists are flesh-eating in a moderate way, their strictest and holiest men, their *consecrated ones*, never touch nor taste of animal food. The priests usually wear plain yellow robes; and, as they live upon alms, they are compelled to take what is given them; and this sometimes consists in part of animal food. They eat it not from choice, but rather from necessity. If the animal was killed especially for *them* they would not taste it.

The whole spirit of Buddhism is against flesh-eating, because all life is sacred, because of the pain produced in killing animals, and because eating animal food tends to grossness of body and stupidity of mind. Buddhists use no strong drinks or liquors. The priests generally eat but one meal a day, and that in the forenoon. Should they eat two, they would partake of them both before the sun had passed the noon-day meridian. The afternoons and evenings they devote to works of charity, to prayer, and meditation.

THE DEATH OF GUATAMA BUDDHA.

The general testimony of scholars, as well as the histories of the Siamese, Birmese, and Singhalese, unite in the opinion that Sakya-Muni Guatama Buddha died a natural death, at the age of about eighty years, the event occurring during the reign of Adzatathat. His body, on the eighth day after its death, was burned, and during the time of the cremation the "nats," exalted intelligences in the heavenly world, hovering over the corps, discoursed sweet music, and threw down upon the asser bl je delicious perfumes.

According to the books and the legends of the East, Buddha not only wrought such marvellous works as healing the sick by a single touch, controlling the elements, sailing through the air attended by his *Rahans*, and visiting other worlds, but he foresaw and prophetically announced his approaching end. Accordingly, Bishop Bigandet, who frequently speaks of Buddha's entering into a state of trance, informs us that when the great sage, weary and worn, had reached Weluwa he was taken with a painful sickness. But says the Bishop, "knowing that this was not the place he was to select for his last moments, he overcame the evil influences of the illness, and entering soon into a state of absolute trance, he remained there for awhile. Awakening from this situation, he appeared anew with his usual state of strength."[*] But the infirmities of age were upon him. And though nominally in his body, he lived upon the verge of Heaven. When sitting one day under the sala-trees to give dying advice to Ananda, it was announced that

---

[*] Bigandet's Life of Buddha, p. 261.

Thoubat wished to see him. He was admitted to Buddha's presence to converse upon religion. After a few moments, as was his custom, of quiet contemplation, Buddha said, "I have spent fifty-one years following the ways of Ariahs, the ways of self-denial and good works, observing the wheel of the law. These lead to Nirvana. To follow the path is to become a Buddha, and *all* may become Buddhas. For twenty-nine years up to this moment I have striven to obtain the supreme and perfect science. I have attained it. I am at peace." Approaching his closing hours and calling Ananda and the Rahans, he said, "When I shall have disappeared from this state of existence and be no longer with you, do not believe that the Buddha has left you and ceased to dwell among you...Do not think, therefore, nor believe that the Buddha has disappeared, and is no more with you." Ananda was Buddha's cousin, and their mutual love was excelled only by that existing between John and Jesus. In the true harmonial man, intellect and affections balance. Buddha's last hours were spent in preaching, and in counselling his friends upon those great spiritual themes that had occupied the prime and the setting years of his life. He passed away in the morning—a morning whose sun can know no setting.

THE BUDDHIST CONTROVERSY.

As held at Pantura, near Colombo, Ceylon,

On Tuesday, 26th August, 1873.

Those who are acquainted with the every day village life in Ceylon can form no idea of the appearance Pantura presented on the occasion of the great controversy between the Protestants and Buddhists. The time appointed for commencing the discussion was eight o'clock in the morning, and long before that hour thousands of natives were seen wending their way, attired in their gayest holiday suits, into the large enclosure in which stood the ample bungalow where the adversaries were to meet. By seven the green was one sea of heads. Each district had sent its quota of villagers, and Colombo was represented by a few intellectual looking, silk-garbed young Singhalese, determined to give up all for the great champion of Buddhism—*Migettuwatte.*

The Protestant party too was very strong. From Monday, catechists and clergymen of every denomination, Baptist, Wesleyan and Church Missionary, flocked from various parts of the Island into the large house prepared for them, one of them, an Oriental scholar of some note, leaving the itinerating work in the wilds of Anoorajapoora, to take part in this important discussion, and assist the Protestant spokesman—Rev. David Silva. The temporary building, the scene of this polemical strife, was a neat cadjan-roofed structure with a raised platform, and parted off in the middle: one portion was occupied by the Rev. David Silva and his party, and the other by the Rev. Mohattiwatte Gunanda, commonly known as *Migettuwatte,* and about 200 priests. An attempt had been made *to* ascertain the numerical strength of each faction, by parting off the compound, by a fence put up in a line with the partition of the platform on which the reverend gentlemen sat, but the increasing numbers prevented the arrangement being carried out. The bungalow itself presented a very gay appearance; the half of it occupied by the Protestant party was decorated with ever-greens, and had a ceiling and cloths on the table as white as snow. The Buddhists, however, went in for more colour; they had rich damask table covers, a ceiling which reminded one of the tri-colour flag of the French, and festoonings of variegated hues, in addition to the yellow silk or satin robes of the priests themselves. These were not all. A *posse* of the Ceylon Police were also there, officered by Inspector Ekenayeke, who was in his uniform; gloved, belted, and mounted on his noble steed, he was seen drilling a handful of police—some fourteen men—and performing all sorts of evolutions amongst the crowds; but the order and quietness which prevailed amongst the five or six thousand men were not due to their presence, as was evidenced in more than one instance during the meeting.

All this, the yellow robed priests, the sable attire of the Protestant clergymen, the fantastic dresses of the immense multitude, the Inspector stalking perfectly erect on the walk lined on each side by children of all ages and complexions, the slow murmur of human voices rising at times like the waves of the ocean, interspersed occasionally by the clear voices of the ubiquitous sherbet-vendor, and the roasted gram seller—the invariable concomitants of a Ceylon crowd—rendered the scene perfectly picturesque. Larger crowds may often be seen in very many places in Europe, but surely such a motley gathering as that which congregated on this occasion can only be seen in the East. Imagine them all seated down and listening with wrapt attention to a yellow robed priest, holding forth from the platform filled with Buddhist priests, clergymen, and Singhalese clad in their national costume, and your readers can form some idea—a very faint one indeed—of the heterogeneous mass that revelled in a display of Singhalese eloquence seldom heard in this country.

So much for the general appearance of the scene; and

now a few words concerning the speakers—at least concerning one of them—the Buddhist priest, Migettuwatte—as he is comparatively unknown to very many. He is a well-made man of apparently forty-five or fifty years of age, rather short, very intellectual looking, with eyes expressive of great distrust, and a smile which may either mean profound satisfaction or supreme contempt. Years ago, owing to some differences with his *confrères,* he left the sect to which he belonged, and established a temple of his own at Cottanchina (in close proximity to St. Thomas' College, Mutwal, and commenced, with the aid of a well educated native, regularly delivering a series of lectures, and publishing, in a printing press established by himself, pamphlets against Christianity. The Wesleyans, the only denomination who ever took the trouble to come forward in defence of the religion of Christ, held various meetings, and the addresses delivered by the learned Pali scholar, Rev. Silva, the Rev. Perera and Mr. John Perera at these gatherings, to the substance of whose speeches permanence was subsequently given in the several periodicals issued by this Society, terminated this quiet controversy in about the year 1867. The desirability of personal argument, however, occurred to the minds of the disputants only a few years afterwards, and the Baddegame monster meeting, in which the Church missionaries took a leading part, was the first important assembly of the kind ; but as on that occasion the discussion was entirely carried on in writing, no opportunity was afforded to the general public of judging of the comparative merits of the leading men of the two parties. On the present occasion no such conditions hampered the disputants. Each man was allowed one full hour to speak, and either to expose the unsoundness of the opponent's religion, or to reply to his adversary's strictures, or both.

As the Rev. David Silva was the first to make some statements adverse to Buddhism, in one of a series of sermons which he was then preaching in the Pantura Wesleyan Chapel, to which Migettuwatte took exception, and denounced as untrue, and the accuracy of which he called upon any Christian to establish, he (Mr. Silva) was asked to open the proceedings by stating his arguments against Buddhism.

The proceedings commenced each day at 8 A.M., and closed at 10; they were again resumed at 3 in the afternoon, and terminated at 5 o'clock; and as only two days were fixed for the controversy, each speaker thus had four hours. The Buddhist priest, it will be seen, had by this arrangement the privilege of having the last word, no mean privilege on any occasion, and to such a consummate master of public speaking as Migettuwatte the advantages of this position were incalculable. The Christian advocate—Mr. Silva—is a learned and fluent speaker: full of Pali and Sanscrit, he addressed the audience as if each of his hearers was a James Alwis, a Louis Zoysa, a Childers, or a Max Müller; he was never at a loss for words, but he forgot that the powers of comprehension in his audience were limited, and that the abstruse metaphysics of Buddha and the learned disquisitions on *The Skandhas, Ayatanas, and Patichasamuphada*, in which he seems to be quite at home, are not adapted to the capacities of his hearers. It is doubtful whether there were even thirty out of the five or six thousand who were present at this controversy who even understood the ornate, though chaste and classic language in which his explanations of these almost incomprehensible subjects were couched, much less the subjects themselves. His renderings of the Pali extracts may be correct, but who was to judge of this? Certainly not the peasantry who hailed from the jungles of Raigam and Pasdoom Corles. Even the Christian party was so conscious of this error of judgment, if nothing more, that they felt chagrined; and several gave vent to their opinions in rather forcible language at the apparent success of the Buddhists on the first day. The Rev. Migettuwatte Gunanda is just the reverse of this. He adapts himself to the capabilities of his audience, and uses the plainest language that the proper treatment of the subjects will allow. Laughing at the idea of Mr. Silva, who in his opinion has only a mere smattering of Pali, attempting to translate difficult extracts from works in that language, he gets over difficulties by arguments more plausible than sound. Of all the weak points in Protestantism, he only touches upon those which will excite the ridicule of the people and evoke a smile of derisive contempt, and winds up a very effective speech, rendered the more attractive by motions made with consummate skill, with a brilliant peroration to which the "great unwashed" listen with deep attention, and the accents of which ring in their ears for some minutes after delivery.

Amongst those present in the bungalow we noticed the Revs. S. Langdon, R. Tebb, S. Coles, C. Jayesinghe, P. Rodrigo, Jos. Fernando, L. Nathanielsz, O. J. Gunasekara, J. H. Abayasekara, H. Martensz, H. Silva, Juan de Silva, D. Fonseka, S. Soysa Modliar, Dr. Staples, Proctors Jayesinghe, Daniel, and Alwis, and a host of catechists and others. Supporting the Buddhist champion were the learned High Priest of Adam's Peak, Sipkaduwe Sumangaabhildhana, Bulatgama Dhammalankara Sri Sumanatissa, Dhammalankara, Subhuti, Potuwilla Indajoti, Koggala Sanghatissa, Amaramoli, Gunaratana, and Weligame Terunanses,—the ablest Oriental scholars amongst the Buddhist priests of this Island.

REV. DAVID DE SILVA'S FIRST SPEECH.

Two minutes before the appointed hour, the Rev. C. Jayesinghe (C.M.S.) stepped forward, and in a very few words, begged the audience to give that attention and quiet hearing to what Rev. Mr. Silva had to say which the importance of the matters he would touch upon deserved. In behalf of the Buddhists, the aged priest "Bulatgame" followed in the same strain; and hoped that the speakers would not forget to use temperate language during the discussion.

Precisely as the clock struck eight, the Rev. David de Silva rose to address the crowd. He stated that before engaging in the controversy it was necessary to explain the reasons for holding it. On the 12th of June last he delivered a lecture in the Wesleyan Chapel, Pantura, on the teachings of Buddha with reference to the human soul : on the 19th of the same month it was taken exception to by the Buddhist party, and denounced as untrue. The present occasion was, therefore, appointed to shew that the doctrine of Buddhism was with reference to the soul, and he hoped that the Buddhist party would, if possible, meet his argument properly ; and that the assembly would judge for themselves what statements were to be received as sound.

He stated that Buddhism taught that man had no soul, and that the identical man received not the reward of his good or bad actions.

According to Buddhism, the *sattá*, sentient beings, are constituted in the five *khandhâs*, namely *rupâk-khandha*, the organised body, *wedanâk-khandha*, the sensations, *sannak-khandha*, the perceptions, *sankharak-khandha*, the reasoning powers, and *winnanak-khandha*, consciousness. In proof of this, he quoted the following from Sanyouttanikaya, a section of Buddha's sermons, and from the Sutrapitaka.

Panehime khikkhave khande desissami Panchupadanakkh ne ca tain sunatha katameca bhikkhave pancakkhanda yam kínchi bhikhhave rupam atitanagata pachcuppannam ajjhattain ia bahiddha va olarikain va sukhumam va hinain va panitam va yam dure va santike ra ayam vuchehati rupvkkhando.

Priests, I will declare the five Khandhas and the five Up-adanakkhandas ; hear it, Priests, what are the five Khandhas? Priests, the body, whether past, future, or present, whether intrinsic or foreign, whether gross or minute, base or excellent, remote or near, this is called Rupak-khandha, the material form.

So of *Wedana*	*Ya kaci bhikkhave vedana*
So of *Sanna* ·	*Ya kaci bhikkhave sanna*
So of *Sankhara*	*Ya kaci bhikkhave sankhara*
So of *Winnana*	*Yan bhikkhave vinnanan*

The same is said of the *Upadanakhanda*, cleaving *Khandhas*.

Katame ca bhikkhave pancupanakkhandha ? Yan kinc, bhikkhave rupan ahtanagata paccuppanan, etc., etc.

Priests, what are the five *Upadanak-khandas?* Priests, the rupa, whether past, future, or present, whether intrinsic or extrinsic, whether gross or minute, base or excellent, remote or near, that is called *rupapadanak-khanda.* So of *Wedana, Sanna, Sankhara,* and *Winnana.*

Yehi keci bhikkhave Samana va Brahmana va aneke vihitan attanan Samanupassamana Samanupassanti Sabbe'te pancupada-nakkhandhe Sammanupassati.

Priests, any priest or Brahmin looking to one's variegated self sees anything, all that, are seen in the five cleaving khandas.

Also from the following verse from *Kawyasekara*, the best Elu poetical work extant.

Paskanda sa kelese
Duknam weya emese
Ru weyin sanrese.
Satara vinnena namin mepase.

The five defiled *khandhas* constitute sorrow; they are, *rupa, wedana, sanna, sankhara,* and *winnana.*

This same individual, it was declared, was comprised in the twelve *Ayatanas,* organs, *Chakkha-yatana,* the eye, *sota-yatana,* the ear, *ghana-yatana,* the nose, *Jiwha-yatana,* the tongue, *Kaya-yatana,* the body, *mana yatana,* the mind with their *bahiddha-yatana,* external aya-tanas, *rupa,* bodily form, *sadda,* sound, *gandha,* odour, *rasa,* flavour, *potthabba,* touch, and *dhamma,* events. The following extracts will bear out this statement.

Katamauca bhikkhave salayatanan, cakkhayatanan sotayatanam ghanayatanam jiwhayatanam kayayatanam manayatanam.

Priests, what are the six ayatanas? the ear, the nose, the tongue, the body and the mind.

Sabham vo bhikkhave desissami, tam sunatha. Kimca bhikkhave sabbam? Cakkhunceva rupanca, sotanca, saddanea, ghananea, ghandnea jivhaca rasaea, kayaca potthabbaca, manoca, dhammaca; idam vuccati bhikkhave sabbam.

Priests, I will preach to you *sabban,* the whole; hear ye, priests, what is the whole? the eye and the bodily form, the ear and the sound, the nose and the odour, the tongue and the flavour, the body and the touch, the mind and the events. Priests, this is called the whole.

Again according to the following authorities, *nama* and *rupa* constituted the whole man.

Katamauca bhikkhave nama rupan wedana sanna cetana phasso manesikaro; idam vuccati namam. Cattaroca maha bhutaca catunnaca maha bhutanam upadaya rupam. Idam vuccati rupam.

Priests, what are the *nama rupa, wedana,* sensation, *sanná,* perception, *chetana*, the faculty of reason, *phasso*, touch, and *manasikaro*, mental objects? this is called the *nama*. That which is compounded of these four elements is called *rupa*.

Tattha katamam namam ? Wedanakkhandho, sannakkdandho, sankharakkhandho Idam vuccatinamam.

What is *nama* ? sensation, perception, and discrimination. Again, in the *Milindaprasne* it is stated.

Yam olarikain etam rupam, ye sukkuma citta cetacika dhamma eatam namam.

Anything gross, that is *rúpa*, anything small, the mind and thoughts, these are *nama*. Thus the first four *Khandhas* evidently are mentioned as constituting *nama rupa*. But from the following quotation it would appear that the fifth *khandha*, consciousness, could not exist independently of the four former.

Yo bhikkhave evam vadeyya aham anna rupeya annatha vedanayn annatha sannaya annatha sankharehi vinnanassa agatini va gatini va cutini va appathne va vuddim va virulhim va vepulldin va pannapessamiti n etam thanam vijjati.

Priests, if anyone say I will shew the arrival and the departure, the death and the birth, the growth, the amplification, and the full development of *vinnana*, consciousness independent of body or of sensation or of perception or of discrimination, the cause is not as he states it, *i.e.*, it is not true, thus shewing that consciousness must be included with the other four *khandhas*.

Again, from the following quotations from the comment of *Wibhanga* it would appear that all the five *khandhas* come into existence together and at the same time:—

Gabbha seyyaka sattanam hi patis patisandhikkhane pancakkhandha apachcha apure ekato pátubhavanti.

Beings conceived in the womb, at the moment of conception the five *khandhas* come into existence; neither before nor after, they come into existence together.

Evaeme gabbhaseyyaânan patisandhikkhandhane pancakkhandha paripunna honti.

Thus, those that are conceived, at the moment of conception the five *khandhas* are perfect.

And also from the following verse from Kawyasekara.

Nam ru deka hera
Neta an pugul behera
Pevata deka nohera
Siyalu katayutu veya nitora.

Besides *nama ruma* there is nothing else that constitutes the individual; by these two in connection at all times everything proper is performed.

Thus is proved that the whole individual is constituted in the five *khandhas*, or in the twelve *ayatanas* or in *nama rupa*.

Now from the following extracts it will be seen that Buddha denies the existence of a soul either in the *Khandhas* or *Ayatana.*

Rupam bhikkhave anattam, yadanattam n'etam mama n'eso 'hamasmin paneso attati.

Organised form, Priests, is not self, that which is not self is not mind, I am not that, that is, not to me a soul.

So of *Wedana, Sanna, Sankhara*, and *Winnana.*

The same is said of rupa, present, past, and future, etc.

Yam kanci rupam atitanagata paccuppannam ajjhattam va bahiddha va olarikam va sukhumam va hinam va panitam va yam dúre va santike va sabbam rupam n'etam mama n'eso 'hamasmi nameso attati cvametam yathabutam sammappanaya datthabbam.

The body, whether past, future, or present, whether belonging to the individual or to others, whether gross or minute, base or excellent, remote or near, all that body is not mine, is not myself, that is not my soul.

So of *Wedana, Sanna, Sankhara, Winnana.*

It is also stated, as will be seen from the following extracts, that the very cause of the *Khandhas* was soulless and that there was no soul to be found :—

Rupam bhikkhave anattamopi hetu yopi paccayo rúpassa uppadaya sopi anattam anattasambhutam rupam kuto attambhvissati.

Priests, body is not a soul; if there be any cause or *paccayo* (that on account of which the thing is produced) for the production of the body, that too is soulless; when the body is soulless whence can there be a soul?

So of *Wedana, Sanna, Sankhara, Winnana.*

The same is stated respecting the *ayatanas;* they are soulless, and in them there was no soul to be found. The following texts will bear out this statement.

Cakkhum bhikkhave anattam yopi hetu yopi paccaya cakhhussa uppadaya sopi anattam anattasambhutam bikkhave cakkhum kuto uttam bhavissati.

Priests, the eye is not a soul; if there be any cause or sequence for the production of the eye, that too is soulless; when the eye is soulless whence can there be a soul?

So of *sota,* ear, *ghana,* nose, *jivha,* tongue, *kaya,* figure, *mano,* mind.

In defining death, it is stated—

Katamanca bhikkhave maranam? Yam tesam tesam sattanam tamha tamha satta nikaya cuti cavanta bhedo antaradhanam maccu maranam kalakiriya khandhanam bhedo, kalebarassa nikkhepo. Idam ruccati maranan.

Priests, what is death? It is the cessation of existence in each state, the breaking up of the frame, the vanishing of its parts, the destruction of the body, decease, the breaking up of the *Khandhas,* the throwing away of the lifeless frame—this is death.

In the advice given by Buddha to the priests to cast away all desire the following passage occurs:—

Yo bhikkhave rupasmin chandarago tam pajahatha, evam tam rupam pahinam bhavissati ucchinna mulam talavatthu katam anabhava katam ayatim anuppada dhammani.

Priests, put off attachment to the body; thus that material form will cease to be, will be cut up by the roots, be eradicated, be reduced to non-existence, prevent future birth.

In the *Mahapadhana suttam* it is stated—

Yam kinci samudaya dhammam tam nirodha dhammam; that which comes into existence will cease to be.

From these authorities it is clear that Buddhism teaches that everything which constitutes man will cease to be at death, and that no immortal soul existed therein, and if then man was only a brute what need had he of a religion? can he possess any moral principle?

Thus if the *Khandhas, Ayatanas,* and *Nama* and *Rupa* constituted the whole of man, and if Buddha himself denied the existence of *Atma* in either of these constituents, and distinctly declared that these would be completely broken up, it followed that there was no *Atma* or soul, which survived the body, but that the human being was on a par with the frog, pig, or any other member of the brute creation. If this were so, and nothing remained of the present man, any being which would exist hereafter and suffer punishment or reap the rewards for the actions committed in this world, which the Buddhists say would be the case, must be a different being, and could not by any possibility be the identical person who committed those actions. And this led the learned lecturer to the second point on which he proposed to speak, but before entering it, he would quote a few authorities from the Holy Scriptures to shew his hearers why the Christians believed in the existence of a soul. The attempt made by the Buddhists to controvert these distinct declarations, contained in the Bible, with reference to the soul, was as futile and silly as the attempt of a small child to conceal the bright rays of the sun by the aid of a lighted candle. He would now refer them to the following passages from " God's Bible," which he likened unto the noon-day sun.

And Jesus said unto him, Verily I say unto thee, To-day shalt thou be with me in Paradise. Luke xxiii. 43.

And he kneeled down, and cried with a loud voice, Lord, lay not this sin to their charge. And when he had said this, he fell asleep. Acts vii. 60.

For I verily, as absent in body, but present in spirit, have judged already, as though I were present, concerning him that hath so done this deed. 1 Cor. v. 3.

And now with reference to the second point, that it was not the identical person who committed good or bad that received the reward or suffered punishment, he would quote the following passages from *Samyutta nikaya.*

Kinnukho bho Gotamá so karoti so patisamvediyatiiti so karoti so patisanvedeyatiti Brahmana, ayam eko anto.

What Gotama (asks a Brahmin) does he who commits the action reap its reward. Brahmin the thought that he who commits the action reaping its reward is one extreme (*i.e.*, a mistake).

Again, King *Milinda* asked *Nagasena* the following question :—

Atthi koci satto imamha kaya annani sankamatiti ?

Is there any being who transmigrates from this body to another body? to which Priest *Nagasena* gave this reply :—

Nahi maha raja, imena pana maha raja namarupeua kammam karoti sobhanam va papakam va ; tena kammeuu annam namarupam patisandahatiti.

No, great King, by these *nama* and *rupa* good or evil actions are performed, and in consequence of these actions another *nama* and *rupa* is conceived.

Again, the following passages occurred in one of the comments :—

Atita bhave kamma paccayena nibbatta te khandha tattheva nruddha atita bhavato imam bhavam agato eka dhammampi natthi.

Those *Khandhas* which came into existence in consequence of actions in a previous state of existence, there itself they ceased to be. There is not one thing which has come to this state of existence from the past state.

Sattena kata kamma paccaya nubhavena anapac chinna kilesa bala vinamitam annam namarupam patubhavati.

"In consequence of the power of actions performed by beings bent by the influence of successive defilement a different *nama rupa* comes into existence."

Again, defining what birth was, in various parts of Buddhist literature there are statements such as the following :—

Katamanca bhikkhava jati! Yaca tesam tesam sattanam tamhi tamhi satta nikaye sanjati okkanti abhinnibbatti khandhanam patubhavo ayatananam patilabho ayam vuccati bhikkhave jati.

Priests, what is birth? It is the production, the conception, coming into existence in such and such state, the appearance of the *Khandhas*, and the development of *Ayatanas.* Priests, this is called birth.

Speaking of *Khandhas* and *Ayatanas*, it is said :—

Uppattikkhane patubhavanti—come into existence at the very moment birth takes place.

He asked whether this, being the proper Buddhist doctrine as expounded in their books, it was likely that the actions of any human being would be influenced by it. If the doctrine were true, it was clear that those who performed meritorious actions would not be benefited, for even supposing that there were any rewards, the doer would not reap them but another. Besides, was it at all to be expected that a man who believes his end to be similar to that of a dog, or a frog, would care what actions he committed? Is not the greatest inducement held out to the murderer, the thief, and the voluptuary to carry on their unlawful pursuits? What mattered it to them how evil their actions were? They would not be punished in a future life; some other beings would be; but how did that in any way affect them? Within man there is a deep-rooted conviction that he will have to suffer for his mis-deeds. This conviction, or conscience, was not confined to a single individual, or a particular race or class of men; it was a general feeling, and does not this doctrine of Buddha belie the convictions implanted in the heart of every man? nay, in the heart of every Buddhist? Besides, was it possible to imagine a dogma more prolific of baneful influences or a greater incentive to evil than this held by the Buddhists, not to mention how iniquitous and contrary to all principles of justice it was to punish one for the misconduct of another. What villain will not exult in the idea that he is not to suffer for what he does in this life! He would challenge the opposite party to adduce a single passage where this *personal* punishment was even declared: if no authority existed where this doctrine was plainly stated, he would, as an indulgence, allow them to point out any passage from which this most salutary doctrine could even be *inferred*. He knew it was impossible. In order to mislead the ignorant, the opposite party might produce metaphors, but in a logical argument metaphors are of no weight, and the metaphors when introduced would, he was sure, be found to prove nothing. The identical wrong-doer, according to the Buddhists, never suffered for his misdeeds. They denied the existence of an

Atma (soul), and both these doctrines only shewed that no religion ever held out greater inducements to the unrighteous than Buddhism did. He then lastly implored the audience, in the name of the Almighty, to carefully and without prejudice weigh the replies that would be tendered, and to hold fast, even at the risk of their lives, that which was true. Before closing, he thanked the audience—fully 5,000 men—for the quiet and attentive manner in which they had listened to him.

REV. MIGETTUWATTE'S FIRST SPEECH IN REPLY.

The Priest Migettuwatte (*Mohattiwatte Gunanda*) then commenced his reply. He said that much penetration was not needed to form a correct opinion of the Rev. Mr. Silva's lecture to which they had all listened. It was a very desultory and rambling speech, which he was certain nobody understood. In his exposition of the Pali extracts, made from Buddha's discourses, he was not more successful, because he completely failed to convey to those present the correct meaning in intelligible language. A *very few* of his audience, however, doubtless perceived that the main argument of the lecture was to shew that because at a human being's death here, his *Pancaskhandha* is completely destroyed, therefore the being who was produced from it in another world was a wholly different being. This was not so. Though the being was not the same, it was not a different one, as he would presently shew. *Atma* (the soul; the living principle) was not an easy subject to explain, but because it was so abstruse it did not follow that its existence was denied. Of course they did not agree with the Christians' view of the soul: this declared that *without any change* man's soul goes to a state of misery or bliss according to its deserts; if so, it must be the human soul with all its imperfections that goes to heaven. For instance, when the Rev. Mr. Silva leaves Pantura for Wellawatta he does not become a different person; it is the same clergyman, and he is known by the same name; and if the human *Atma* goes to heaven that *Atma* must be human still, and the being who enjoys bliss—a man!

And now it behoved him to explain this important doctrine
of *Pancaskhandha*, in the expounding of which the rev.
gentleman, owing to his superficial knowledge of Pali, had
made such mistakes.

In doing so, he would take good care not to use language
that seemed like Latin and Greek to the multitude; and he
left to his learned coadjutors to judge of the correctness of
his interpretation of these doctrines. The great Buddha's
last discourse, in which man's nature was explained, was not
one that could be comprehended by everybody, and much
less by a clergyman of Mr. Silva's linguistic attainments. It
was perfectly true, according to Buddhist doctrines, to say
that at man's death no portion of *Pancaskhandha* was transferred to another world; yet the being who was produced at
death in consequence of existence here was not a *different*
being. This was not a new interpretation of the doctrine.
He could assure his hearers that this construction was
admitted to be the correct and proper one at several meetings,
held hundreds of years ago for the very purpose, in which
the most erudite of the age took part, whose knowledge of
Pali, it was needless to say, was far superior to that of the
rev. gentleman who had just spoken. The whole of Buddha's
doctrines were written in Pali, and no person having an
imperfect knowledge of that language could be expected to
understand those abstruse sayings. He would now shew the
extent of the rev. gentleman's Pali attainments, and
fortunately for him, he had in his possession a little publication
which greatly facilitated this task. This *brochure*, entitled
Granthasekara, was published by Mr. Silva, and in it occurs a
short Pali verse of four lines giving the substance of a passage
in the New Testament, of which the first line even contains
several egregious blunders. For instance, in the sentence
commencing with "*Tava namo paviththo hothu*" it was quite
erroneous to use the aspirate *paviththo*. There was no such
word as *paviththo* in the Pali language; it ought to have
been *pavitto*, and in *Tava namo* it was equally wrong to have
used the masculine termination. If the rev. gentleman was
not competent to connect two Pali words agreeably to
grammatical rules, but committed so many blunders in those

few lines of Pali, his hearers would be able to judge of his fitness to explain the great Buddha's abstruse metaphysics found only in works written in that language. The assembled multitude may not know whether his (the Priest's) criticism of the rev. gentleman's grammatical constructions was correct or not; but if he were wrong, there was no doubt that the priests well versed in Pali literature who surrounded him, would correct him. To the learned it certainly was amusing to hear the rev. gentleman, with such an imperfect knowledge of Pali, attempting to explain the difficult doctrine of *Pancaskhandha*.

Pancaskhandha, then, consists of the five components,— *Rupaskhandha*, the body. 2. *Wedanaskhandha*, sensation. 3. *Sannaskhandha*, perception. 4. *Sanskharaskhandha*, discrimination; and 5. *Winnanaskhandha*, external consciousness. It was well known that at man's death *Rupaskhandha*, or the body, was consigned to the grave, and that *Wedanaskhandha*, or physical sensation, ceased to exist. So they may be quite sure that no part of these two *Skhandhas* ever went to another world to enjoy bliss or suffer punishment. In like manner, the remaining three *Skhandhas*, too, ceased to exist at man's death; and neither did they suffer in a future existence the consequences of acts done in this life. But yet the being who is produced simultaneously with the extinction of *Pancaskhandha* was not a different being. He would try to make this doctrine yet clearer. The much revered Bible of the Christians was not the original Bible written by Moses and others, and in use amongst the primitive believers of Christ; and yet they could not say it was a different Bible. The substance in both was the same, though it was *not* the identical book: so it was with *Atma*. Though at one's death all those constituents which make up the outward physical man perish, and no portion of them is transferred to another world, yet the conscious being, though produced in consequence, is not a different one. Accordingly, it was as incorrect to say that it was a different being who suffered for the good or evil committed here, as to assert that it was the *identical* doer with all his environments who thus suffered. He (the Priest) hoped that his illustration of the Bible would

3

have enabled his auditory to more fully comprehend this abstruse doctrine. The following Pali extract from the *Kattawastu Prakarana* of the *Abhidharma Pitaka* fully bore out the assertion made at the outset of his lecture, that if the human soul participated in a future existence, the conse-quences of acts done in this life, the beings who dwelt in heaven must be men, instead of glorified spirits.

Sv'èva puggalo sandhavati asma loka paran tokan, parasma loka iman lokan 'ti amanta atthi koci manusso hutva devo hoti'ti micca. Sace hi sandhavati sv'eva puggalo ito cuto param lokam anannahevan maranan nahoti'ti panatipato'pinupalabbhati.

"If they say that the same person passes from this world to the other world, or from the other world to this world, then some who having been men become gods, it is false. If this very person passes it is the same man that having died goes from here to the other world, not another, and there is no death, and there will be no killing."

Human beings had two deaths; one was the complete change sensations underwent every moment, which resulted in the production of new emotions; and the other was that death which every body understood by the phrase of "going to another world." Sensations, they were well aware, vary every moment: desires, power of thinking, passions, and opinions change constantly. The body, too, which, according to Buddhism, consisted of thirty-two parts, undergoes, though imperceptibly, the same operation : for instance, hair, which was one of these thirty-two components, grew every day, and its attaining an extraordinary length, when not cut, was only prevented by its occasionally falling off. Accordingly, the hair now on their heads was not the same as that they had when they were infants. This change was not confined to hair; the remaining constituents of the body shared the same fate—*that* of being produced and of perishing every moment. Moreover, the various parts of *Rupaskhandha* (outward appear-ance) were also subject to this momentary death to which allusion was previously made. The proper meaning of the second death, of which he had spoken, was the termination of man's career in this life. Simultaneously with this death, a change of existence, causing the production of a being to whom the quintessence of man's inmost desires was transferred, took place. It was not a new being that was thus produced, as the rev. gentleman had attempted to shew; because the desire producing the being was not a new desire, but only a result of those that preceded it. The origin of the desires was the same, and there was a continuity in them, the quintessence of which only took shape at death. If, as Christians declared, the *Atma* which proceeded to another world were undying, and was not a cleaving to existence, as he had just explained, and which was the view held by the Buddhists, what did the Christians mean by it? Was it matter? had it any shape? was it like an egg, a stick, or a fruit? If it were some *substance* that they meant by *Atma*, surely it would not be difficult to confine it by locking up a dying man in an air-tight chest. Should the Christians fail to explain the exact nature of this *Atma*, that itself would be conclusive evidence to prove there was no *Atma* that travelled to another world. The doctrine of the being that is produced at death has been propounded to the Buddhists in the words *na ca so, na ca anno.* By *na ca so* was meant that it was not the same being, and *na ca anno* signified that it was not another. He could give abundant authorities in support of his positions, but he thought he had sufficiently clearly explained to the assembly that though the conscious being passing into another world was not the same human being that walked this earth, yet it was not another; and so it was most incorrect to say that it was a different person that suffered in a future existence for the misdeeds committed in this, or that the existence of a living principle was denied by them (the Buddhists), as the rev. gentleman had attempted to prove.

He (the Priest) would now bring this portion of his argument to a close, as he was sure he had completely refuted the arguments adduced against Buddhism to the entire satisfaction of his auditory. He had much more to say, however, in regard to the same subject, but he would defer further remarks to the subsequent occasions during which he would have the privilege of addressing them.

And with reference to Christianity, the Priest went on to

say that the Christian was not a true religion, and by embracing it no being can thereby hope to enjoy bliss in a future life. Out of the many errors with which Christianity teemed, he would point out a few, which would conclusively shew that *that* religion was not worthy of credence.

In the first place, Christians, wherever they went, commenced propagating their religion by giving the object of their worship the name of a being already held in veneration by the nations amongst whom they intended preaching the Gospel; for instance, in Calcutta, Christ was called Son of *Iswara*, which would be seen from the words, *Iswaryna sute Khriste*, to occur in a Sanskrit stanza. This was done in the view of enlisting the sympathies of the Hindus, who held the god *Iswara* in great reverence. And in Ceylon, *Jehovah* went by the name of "*Dewiyanwahanse*," as this term existed amongst the Singhalese to denote the gods in whom they believed. It would thus be seen that the Christians adapted themselves to different nations with the view of deceiving them. Again in Exod. xx. 5, the words used for "jealous God" did not express the meaning conveyed in the original. The word "*jevalita*" which appeared in the Singhalese Bible, meant glittering, or luminous, but the English word "jealous" did not mean anything of the kind; the proper synonym for it would have been envious, for what was jealousy but envy? If the word "envy" had been used by the translators, there would have been no chance of deceiving the people, for who would have believed in an *envious* God? and that was the reason for giving such an interpretation to the English word "jealous." He could assure his hearers that deceit was habitually practised by the Christian teachers with the view of gaining converts, and in hopes that even such a course would help their cause. They were also in the habit of omitting portions of Scripture whenever it suited their purpose; for instance, in the edition of the Scriptures published in 1840 by the very Society to which the rev. gentleman belonged, the passage, "And they shall no more offer their services unto devils after whom they have gone a whoring," appeared in Lev. xvii. 6, but in the later edition published by the same Society a gross deception had been practised by leaving those words out. Possibly the Christians were ashamed that it should be known that they had offered sacrifices to devils, and had omitted this passage from the second edition. He was surprised at this omission. Who had the right to omit or add a verse at pleasure to a book for which a Divine origin was claimed? If such omissions were made in one portion, what was to prevent garbled accounts appearing in other parts of the Bible? This habit of adding to, and omitting from, the Bible was very common amongst Protestants, but he was glad to say that it was not so with the Roman Catholics, to whom great praise was due for never altering their Bibles.

Further, in Gen. vi. 6, speaking of Jehovah, the Creator, it was declared, "And it repented the Lord that he had made man on the earth and it grieved him at his heart." Who usually commit actions for which they have cause to regret afterwards? Was it not ignorant, foolish man alone? and how supremely ridiculous was it for a Creator who was declared to be omniscient to commit any actions for which it was necessary to repent and grieve? If he were omniscient, he ought surely to have seen the consequences of his creating man, on account of which it is said he afterwards repented, and his failing to foresee this result clearly proves that the Christians' God does not possess any such foreknowing power as is attributed to him. How improper was it, then, to believe on such a frail, repenting and grieving being as the Christians' omnipotent God and Creator? Were not they convinced that Jehovah was not omniscient; and further, that he had all the failings of man?

It would also seem that God required some visible means of identifying any required thing, or in other words, that like a blind man he needs a guide; for instance, before the first born of Egypt were killed, it was ordered that blood should be sprinkled on the door posts of the houses of the Israelites, in order to distinguish their houses from those of the Egyptians; for according to Exod. xii. 23, "The Lord will pass through to smite the Egyptians, and when he seeth the blood upon the lentil and on the two side posts, the Lord will pass over the door, and will not suffer the destroyer to come in unto your houses to smite you." This shewed that it was impossible for Jehovah to distinguish the houses of the Israelites without this outward and visible sign: if he were omniscient, surely this was not necessary. What right, then, had they to call this being an omniscient God? He (the Priest) knew that his friend the rev. gentleman would attempt to explain this away by assigning the ridiculous reason of its being a symbol of Christ's death; but he would not let him off with any such puerile reply.

In the command given to Moses in Exod. iv. 6, with reference to the miracles that he was to perform before the King of Egypt, God's orders were to do a certain miracle, and if the Israelites were not given up, to perform a second and so on; but what was the necessity for this conditional order if he were omniscient? He should have certainly known the effect of those miracles if he really were what he was represented to be. Was not imperfect human nature betrayed even in this? The line of conduct of a medical man was precisely similar: if one medicine failed, another was prescribed; this was simply because the medical man was not omniscient, was not certain of the effects of each medicine. What, then, did this incident shew? Simply what he asserted before, namely, that the Creator was not omniscient.

There was another passage in the Bible which would give them an idea of the nature of the God that the Christians believed in; and that was Exod. iv. 24. It was there stated—"And it came to pass by the way in the inn, that the Lord met him, and sought to kill him. Then Zipporah took a sharp stone, and cut off the foreskin of her son, and cast it at his feet, and said, Surely a bloody husband art thou to me. So he let him go." They will here see that the means adopted by Zipporah, when God sought to kill Moses whom he had once chosen as a servant, were not quite unknown to some of *them*. Did it not remind them of the sacrifices usually made to appease the wrath of some other beings whom it was unnecessary to name? What was the procedure adopted by devil *dancers* in this country when any body was afflicted with a disease brought on by the influence of evil spirits? Was it not to shed the blood of a goat or a fowl, as the case might be, by cutting some part of the animal, and offering it to the Devil? The course pursued by Zipporah was just the same, and he would leave them (the crowd) to judge of the nature of the God of the Christians, whose wrath was appeased and Moses saved by throwing the foreskin at his feet.

Again, it appeared from Judges i. 19 that "though the Lord was with Judah when he drove out the *inhabitants* of the mountain, yet he could not drive out the inhabitants of the valley, because they had chariots of iron." This incident was further proof, and a very convincing one, that the God of the Hebrews, whom the Christians adored, was not Almighty; it shewed that he feared iron; and every one there present, the Priest said, knew who were afraid of iron! It was usual amongst the natives of this country to have a small piece of iron when food was carried from one place to another, and when decoctions were prepared it was customary to tie a string with a piece of iron hanging from it round the pot in which is the medicine. This was done to keep away devils and sundry evil spirits; and that was the meaning of the God of the Hebrews fearing iron chariots! It was needless for him to further explain. These facts would greatly assist his auditory to form a correct opinion as to whether the Jehovah of the Christians was the true God or not. In conclusion, the eloquent Priest said that he had explained what the Buddhists meant by *Atma*, and he hoped the rev. gentleman would tell them what Christians meant by a *soul*; and unless Mr. Silva would produce authorities to support his statement that Buddha had likened a human being to a brute, he (the Priest) would consider him as having uttered an untruth. The term *Atma* was used by him, he said, as it was the only word in general use to express the subtle principle or cleaving to existence of which he had been speaking. He had three hours more before him to engage in this controversy, during which he would conclusively shew the truth of Buddhism, and adduce further arguments to prove the falsity of Christianity. After thanking the large audience for having so attentively listened to him, the Priest closed his speech, and immediately the great crowd dispersed.

THE REV. MR. SILVA'S SECOND SPEECH.

At three o'clock—the hour appointed for resuming the controversy—the crowd had increased three-fold; the inhabitants of the neighbouring villages, having heard of the two able and effective speeches of the eloquent disputants, flocked into the green around the bungalow, and by the time the speakers ascended the "rostrum," the din of the thousands of human voices was so great that a severe fight between the two factions was apprehended, but when, in a sharp, but clear voice, the Rev. David Silva commenced to reply, the confusion ceased, and the multitude, at least as many of them as were at a hearing distance, listened with deep attention to the words that fell from the learned speaker.

Mr. Silva said that he would reply in as few words as possible to the strictures made on Christianity, and pass on to point out the very serious defects in the religion professed by his opponent. With reference to the charge that he was ignorant of the Pali language, and which was attempted to be proved by pointing out a passage in a work published by him, he said that if his opponent had taken the trouble to understand the meaning of the title page even of the *Grantha sakera* he would not have made such a miserable exhibition of his ignorance. The misrepresentation of facts by his opponent was either wilful, or done through ignorance; for the title page of the work distinctly stated that the passages therein contained were *selections* made by him from different works. Even if there was an ungrammatically connected passage, *he* was not responsible. The two words on which so much stress had been laid by his opponent were simply reprinted by him from the Burmese Testament, and surely it was not his province, in a work like the one he was engaged in, to correct the misreadings; his object was to make a *few selections* from some standard works, and *nothing more*. So much for his opponent's charge of his ignorance of Pali.

An attempt was also made by his opponent to impugn the honesty of the translators of the Bible, by declaring that a portion of a verse appearing in one edition of the Singha-

Iese Scriptures was wilfully and deliberately omitted in a later one. A greater untruth had never been uttered. There was not one in that assembly competent to question the honesty of the learned translators of the Singhalese Bible. In fact, there was no omission at all, but in order to render the translation as close to the original as possible, a transposition of verses had been made in the second edition different to that in the first; and that was the omission of which his opponent had made so much. He would assure his hearers that it was the love of truth that had actuated the translators, and the charge of dishonesty laid against them would only recoil on his opponent himself. And in regard to his opponent's question, whether it would not be possible to retain what Christians called the soul by locking up a dying man in a closed chest, as even air could be confined, the learned lecturer said that illustration only betrayed the ignorance of his opponent. It was his (the Priest's) impression that there was nothing so fine as air; but he little knew that electricity was so much more subtle than air that it could pierce through any substance, and certainly through an iron chest, in which his opponent had proposed that a dying man should be placed to prevent the soul from escaping from it. The reason for styling Christ Son of *Iswara*, in Calcutta, was not with the view of deceiving the people as his opponent had declared; but as "*Iswara*" meant in the original Sanskrit a being endowed with great power and might, this word was made use of to express these qualities in the great Father of Christ. The meaning attached to the word *Iswara* at the present day is not the one given to it in the *Vedas*, where the term is used to express any being who was chief and lord. With reference to the Singhalese word *Dewyanwahanse*, used by the Christians here to signify the God whom they worship, it was not adopted by them to deceive the people of the land, as his opponent most unjustly asserted, but simply because the language did not afford any better word. He considered it very improper that one so profoundly ignorant of the different senses in which the same word could be used, as his opponent was, should engage in a controversy like the present.

In illustration of the fact that words have different meanings he would quote the following passage from *Vinaya Pitaka* :—

Pandako Bhikkhave anupasampanno, na upasampadetabbo, upasampanno nasetabbo.

An eunuch who was unordained ought not to be ordained. If ordained *nasétabbo.*

The word *nasétabbo* may be translated " ought to be killed;" but Buddha, whose first precept was not to take away life, would not say that the ordained eunuch was "to be killed," or that his neck was to be cut off; at least no sane man will put that construction; what Buddha really said was to disrobe such an one, to excommunicate him; so it was with many words in Scripture. They had more than one meaning. It was so in every language, and his opponent himself whilst discoursing on the soul used the word *Atma* throughout his speech, though he denied its existence altogether; what did he mean by it ?

His opponent had also spoken of God's repentance. The original Hebrew word translated " repentance " in the Singhalese Bible was " *Nokam,*" which did not mean that God had "regretted" for doing anything wrong: and to further elucidate this subject he would read an extract from an article in the Singhalese periodical the *Banner of Truth*—See page 39 in Vol. of 1861. (Vide Appendix A.) As for God's order to mark the door posts of the houses of the Israelites with blood, the lecturer said that was simply a symbol of Christ's death.

The lecturer then passed on to point out the absurdities and contradictions of Buddha's teaching in regard to the origin of animal life, and quoted the following passage from the *Sanyutta nikáya:*—

Katame ca Bhikkhave paticcasamuppade ? Avijja paccaya, Bhikkhave samkhara, samkhara paccaya vinnanam, vinnana paccaya nama rupam, nama rupa paccaya salayatanam, Salayatana paccaya phasso, phassa paccaya vedana, vedana paccaya tanha, tanha paccaya upadanam. upadana paccaya bhavo, bhava paccaya jati, jati paccaya jara maranam soka paridevados dukkha domanass upayasa sambharanti. Evam etassa kevalassa dukkha khandhassa samudayo hoti.

Priests, what is *paticca samuppâda?* On account of ignorance, Priests, *sankhara,* merit and demerit, are produced; on
account of merit and demerit, consciousness, on account of
consciousness, *nama rupa,* on account of *nama rupa,* the six
sensitive organs, on account of the six sensitive organs,
contact, on account of contact, sensation, on account of sensation, desire, on account of desire, cleaving to existence, on
account of cleaving to existence, *bhava,* states of existence, on
account of *bhava,* birth, on account of birth, decay, death,
sorrow, crying, pain, disgust, and passionate discontent.
Thus is produced the complete body of sorrow.

Now *avijja* was *dukkhe annanam dukkha samudaye annanam,*
ignorance of sorrow, ignorance of the producing causes of
sorrow, etc., etc. But what is *dukkha?* It is *jati, jara,
maranam,*—birth, decay, and death; *avijja,* then, is ignorance of
that which did not exist, for *jâti,* birth, is the consequence of
bhava, existence.

In consequence of *avijja, samkhâra* is produced. *Samkhâra*
is the accumulation of *punnabhisamkhara,* merit, and *apunnab-
hisamkhara,* demerit; he who had *vijjá,* clear preception, will
either accumulate merit or demerit, but the Buddhists are
told to perform *kusal,* merit, to accumulate merit; but
according to Buddha's doctrine, the accumulation of merit
was the consequence of ignorance.

Because of *samkhara vinnana,* consciousness is produced.
Now what is *vinnana?* It is *cakkhu vinnanam, sota vinnanam,
ghana vinnanam, jivha vinnanam, kaya vinnanam, mano
vinnanam,* consciousness of the eye, ear, the nose, the tongue,
the body, the mind. But these organs are not yet produced;
they are not in existence; the cause of the *ayatanas,* organs,
being *nama rupa.* Besides it is clearly stated that the *vinnana*
cannot exist independent of *nama rupa,* that all the *khandhas*
must come into existence *paripunna,* perfect, and *ekato,*
together; neither after nor before, *apaccha apure.*

In consequence of *vinnana, nama rupa* are produced,
although the first four *khandas* constitute *nama rupa;* yet

Nam ru deka hera
Net an pugul behera

besides the *nama rupa*, there is no other individual. The whole individual is perfect in *nama rupa*.

In consequence of *nama rupa* the six organs *salayatana* are produced, but *vinnana* was the consciousness of the eye, etc., and the *nama rupa* included the whole individual ; but here the organs are the consequence of the perfect five *khandhas*.

In consequence of the six organs *phassa*, contact, is produced, but *phassa* was included in the *nama* which was the consequence of consciousness. Now it is the consequence of the organs, and the *nama* was contact produced *phassaja*.

In consequence of *phassa*, *vedana*, sensation, is produced, but what is *vedana* ? It is *cakkhu samphassaja vedana*, sensation produced by the contact of the eye ; so of *sotasamphassaja*, *ghana*, *jivaha*, *kaya*, *mano*.

But the *vedana* is included in the *nama* which was produced before the organs were produced, and that as the result of contact. *Tattha katamam namam.* What then is *nama* ? *vedanakkhandho*, sensation, *sannakkhandho*, perception, *samkharakkhandho*, discrimination. If *nama rupa* were the result of *vinnana*, certainly *vedana* could not be the consequence of *phassa*.

In consequence of *vedana tanha*, desire is produced, but *avijja* was ignorance of *dukkha samudaya*, the producing cause of sorrow, which is defined to be, *ya yam tanha ponobhavika nandiraga sahagata tandra tandaja nandini seyyathiidam. kama tanha ; bhava tanha, vibhava tanha.* It is the desire of continued existence and delighting in the enjoyment of that state they now occupy, *i.e.*, desire of pleasure, of continued transmigration, and of annihilation upon death ; so then this *tanha* must exist before one could be ignorant of it.

Now to come to *jati*, the consequent of *bhava;* what is *jati?* It is the *khandhanam patubhavo*, the coming to existence of the *khandhas* and the *ayatanam patilabko*, the development of the organs. But *vinnana* produced *nama rupa*, which in their turn produced the organs; here *bhava* is said to be the antecedent *khandhas* and the *ayatanas*. Hence the great confusion of this so-called, the previously unknown doctrine.

The lecturer then wound up by saying : I divide this large assembly into two classes, the learned and the unlearned, and this subject being indeed a subject for the learned, I beg them to consider whether this fundamental doctrine of Buddha was not an absurdity, and a confusion of thought. Is it not like saying the son is begotten by the father, and the father is begotten by the son, and both have one origin, ignorance ? How absurd is the theory !

THE REV. MIGETTUWATTE'S SECOND REJOINDER. *

The Rev. Migettuwatte, rising, begged of the people to give him a patient hearing, and said that though previously he had styled the gentleman who had just spoken the rev. gentleman, yet he, in his reply, having called him (the Priest) *virudhakaraya,* "the opponent," it was his intention to use the same epithet towards him, and wished his hearers to distinctly understand this. Though the two speakers, belonging to two different religions, had come forward to take part in the controversy, solely with the view of ascertaining which was the true religion, he said that there was no *personal* enmity between them, which the word "opponent or adversary" used by the opposite side would seem to imply, but now that it had been used, he regretted to say he had no other alternative but to do the same.

With regard to the last speech of the Christian party, he would mention that no attempt had ever been made to explain the reason for using the milder word *jwalita* in the Singhalese Bible, thus deceiving the natives of this Island. The word "envy," as he once assured them, was the true meaning of the word "jealous" in the original ; neither did his opponent mention or explain how this jealousy or envy

---

* The Buddhist Priest, Migettuwatte, though a noted Singhalese and Pali scholar, was necessarily troubled at times in finding idiomatic words to convey his meaning. Knowing his deficiency in understanding the genius of the English language, and difficulty in the selection of terms, I have made, by request, some changes. I hope, however, they are to the benefit, rather than to the injury of the Buddhist's arguments.

assigned to the Creator could be reconciled with his other attributes. His opponent knew as well as himself that it was impossible to give a satisfactory reply to these objections, and that was the reason of his silence. His opponent's shirking the responsibility of the work published in his name, which contained several ungrammatical Pali passages, by stating that he was only a compiler, was not satisfactory. If he knew Pali correctly he would not have allowed such an egregious blunder as he had pointed out to creep into his work uncorrected: the passage may have been taken from the Burmese Testament, as was alleged, but that did not the less betray his opponent's ignorance of Pali: it was highly improper that the incorrect passage should have been copied without alteration. The accounting for the omission of a passage in one edition of the Singhalese Old Testament, which appeared in a previous one, by stating that there had been a transposition of verses, was also unsatisfactory. Clearly one or the other of the editions was wrong! If the placing a passage in a certain position correctly expressed the meaning intended to be conveyed, by transposing it a different and an incorrect meaning would be given. Which construction were they to receive as the correct one? And so all his opponent's eulogium as to the honesty of the translators went for nothing. Both sets of translators could not have been either equally honest or learned; if they were, the arrangement of the verses in both the translations would have been the same; the fact was that the Christians *altered* their Bibles whenever they pleased.

Styling Christ "Son of *Isvara*" was attempted to be explained by proving that words had various meanings: but they all knew that this was a very lame defence, and that the true object of the Christians was to deceive, and ingratiate themselves into the favour of the Hindus, who held *Isvara* in reverence. Well, if the Christians' God was *Isvara*, had Jehovah a wife as Isvara is said to have? Umayanganawa was the name of his wife; what was the name of the partner of the Christians' God? Perhaps the Christians themselves did not know. He would enlighten them on a future occasion. What was the reply adduced by his opponent to the remarks made by him upon Gen: vi. 6, wherein it was said that the Lord repented and grieved for having made man on earth? Absolutely nothing. It is true that he had read an extract from an old number of the *Banner of Truth*, a pamphlet published by the Christians in connection with a controversy held on a previous occasion by the same parties, but at that time he had utterly refuted the teachings of the passage, and so what was the use in again reiterating those hackneyed arguments? It was highly improper that that obsolete book should have been brought forward before such an assembly as the present one, as it was no reply at all to his objections. Further, how ridiculous was it to explain away the command to mark the door posts of the houses of the children of Israel with blood, by calling it a symbol of Christ's death. What marking of door posts was there on that occasion, and what a silly reply was this to his argument, that because the Christians' God required an outward and visible sign to distinguish objects, that, therefore, he did not possess the power of knowing everything? Even he (the Priest) was ashamed that such a reply should have been given before such a learned audience. The facts recorded in the Scriptures were clear, that God, seeing the blood, passed over the houses of the Jews; this plainly shewed, as was previously stated, that the Creator required some sign whereby to identify any given thing, and what was the inference to be drawn from this but that Jehovah was not omniscient?

Thus much with reference to those questions that had been answered; but what about the several commands given to Moses in regard to the miracles that he was to perform before Pharaoh, namely, that if he did not succeed with one, then he was to try another, which fact was also mentioned by him to prove, as it plainly did, that God was not omniscient; and what was the reason of the armies of Judah fleeing away from the chariots of iron? How did Christians get over the difficulty arising out of God's injunction to circumcise Moses' son, thereby betraying His fondness for human blood in common with evil spirits having similar tastes, about whom it was unnecessary to give a more detailed account to his auditory? As he had sufficiently clearly explained, on a previous occasion, the reason for the Christians' God fearing iron and of his fondness for human blood, he would not enlarge upon these subjects at present, but the affair of Moses' son would clearly shew them, if any further explanation were at all needed, the reason of this fondness of the Christians' Jehovah for human blood.

And now, what about the *soul* of the Christians? what was it made of? and what was it like, if it did not resemble what the Buddhists meant by *Atma*? None of these questions had even been attempted to be explained: they all knew what that signified.

Lastly, with reference to the Buddhist doctrine of *Pancaskhandha* and man's future, they were not subjects that were intelligible to persons of limited knowledge: the being who would hereafter suffer for actions committed in this life was not the identical one that walked this earth, though it was not a wholly different one, as he had previously shewn; and he would now quote a passage from the Buddhist Scriptures which would more clearly explain to them this abstruse subject. It was this:—

Maranantika vedana santattanam sannipatam asahantassa itape khitta harita tala pattamica kamena upa sussamane sarire naruddhesu cakkhadisu indriyesu hadaya vatthu matte patitthite kayindriya manindriya jivitindriyesu tam khanavasesa hadaya vatthu sannissitam vinnana garu sama sevitasanna pubbakanam annataram laddhavasesa paccaya sankhara sankhatam kamman tadupatthapitam va kamma nimitta gatinimitta sankhatam visayam arabbha parattati taderam parattamanam tanha vijjanam appahinatta avijja paticchadit adinave tasmin visaye tanhanameti sahajata sankhara khipanti santati vasena tanhanamiyamanam sankharehi khippamanam orimatira rukkha vinibaddham rajjumalambitva. Matikatikkamakeriya purimanca nissayaim jahati aparanca kamma samutthapitam nissayam asadayamanam anasadayamanam va arammanadihi eva paccayehi parattati.

As the meaning of the death and regeneration of a being was, in the extract, sought to be conveyed by a familiar illustration, he would give them a free translation of its meaning, and he had no doubt that his auditory would then be able to better comprehend this difficult doctrine. As the newly plucked talipot leaf, when put in the sun, loses its green colour by degrees and assumes a whiteness, so at his death the sentient being gradually loses the use of his physical senses, such as those of seeing and hearing, owing to the pains of death.

While this process of the loss of the use of these senses is going on, three of the senses enter the body and remain attached to the heart. These three are, the sense of feeling, of understanding, and that of life. The sense of feeling is that by which one is enabled to perceive when any object touches the body, the sense of understanding is the power of distinguishing any object, and what is called the inner sense of life is the state of undying existence. At the death of the being with whose heart was associated these three senses, he sees, as if in a dream, that he is engaged in the same actions, whether sinful or righteous, to which he was greatly addicted in this life; for instance, if he had been given up to murder and other heinous crimes all his life through, at his last moments he feels as if he is again committing them, but if his career on earth was a righteous one, as if he had been practising meritorious actions, such as giving alms and observing "*sila*," he perceives at death that he is going through such a holy life over again. If, at one's dying moments, this last scene presents itself, his future state is sure to be a happy one. And it is equally certain that the being who fancies at his death that he is committing immoral actions will be born into a state of misery. The presentment of the nature of the life that the being is in a future state to enjoy, also resembles a dream, that is, he sees the state in which he is to be re-born as if it were in a dream. And as this state, whether happy or miserable, appears in an enchanted form, man, who is full of desires, naturally cleaves to it, and in consequence, immediately after death, realisation takes place in that state of which he had the presentiment. Thus they would see that death and the re-birth of the being are simultaneous. In short, man's actions and desires here affected and regulated his future career, and this cleaving to existence believed in by them (the Buddhists) was according

to the desires indulged by the man in his existence on earth.
Further, no part of man proceeded to another world to be
born again, but simply this cleaving to existence took place
at death, according to the nature of the desires that existed
in him, and therefore to say that the being who suffered
hereafter for actions committed in this world was not the
same but another, was absurd. If any of his auditory had
been present at the bedside of a dying man, they could have
no doubt as to the fact that at the man's death there was
always a presentiment of the future misery or bliss that he
was going to partake of. This found expression, they would
remember, either in hideous groanings or delightful raptures.
For the being who is to be born into a happy state always
sees such pleasant and delightful objects as heavenly
mansions, etc., but he whose future will be misery only sees
the terrors of torments, and his exclamations often clearly
shew to the bystander whether it is a state of misery or bliss
that the man is going to inherit.

The Buddhist doctrine concerning man was " *anamataggo
yam Bhikkhave samsaro pubba koti na pannayati*," etc., that is,
that immortal man had neither a beginning nor an end; and
the Christian Bible, rightly interpreted, supported this view.
Consider the Scriptural account of the creation of man, as contained in Gen. ii. 7: "The Lord God formed man of the dust of
the ground, and breathed into his nostrils the breath of life;
and man became a living soul." There could be no doubt
acording to this account, then, that the spirit breathed into
Adam was a portion of the spirit of God, who was eternal:
thus Adam, or the Adamic form, was made the receptacle of
spirit, was made *eternal*; and if Adam were the father of the
human race, as is alleged, then all men are eternal, and this
was precisely the Buddhist doctrine, according to which, as
previously said, man had not either a beginning or an end.
The only means of terminating this continual round of
existence was by entering *Nirvana*, and which exceptional
consummation—exceptional because eternal existence was
the rule, and man is by nature said to move about in the
anamatagga samsara, or in the immense or unborn and infinite
metempsychosis—was only to be attained by undergoing

great pains, and acting according to, and realising the several results of, the four sublime paths of virtue prescribed by Buddha, namely, *Soran*, *Sakradayami*, *Anagami*, and *Arhat*. A being who walks thus will be saved.

The eloquent Priest, again reverting to Christianity, said that he could cite another instance which shewed that the God whom the Christians worshipped was fond of human sacrifices: namely, the case of Jephthah's daughter, who was, it was declared, sacrificed according to Jephthah's vow.* Though the Protestants tried to make out that it was not literally carried out, yet he would refer to a note against that passage appearing in the Douay Bible, which stated that the sacrifice was made; and here he could not but pass a high

---

* Bishop Colenso, of Natal, an eminent scholar and theologian in the English Church, says (in his Natal Sermons, page 359) that—"It was a common practice among the Jews in the times of Jeremiah and Ezekiel to offer human sacrifices." And he quotes the following, among other Biblical passages, to prove it:—

"And they built the high places of B al. which are in the valley of the Son of Hinnom, to cause their sons and their daughters to pass through the fire unto Moloch; which I commanded them not."—Jer. xxxii. 35.

"Then he took his eldest son, that should have reigned in his stead, and offered him for a burnt-offering upon the wall."—II. Kings iii. 27.

"For the children of Judah have done evil in my s ght, saith the Lord; they have set their abomination, in the house which is called by My name, to pollute it; and they have built the high places of Tophet, which is in the valley of the Son of Hinnom, to burn their sons and their daughters in the fire, which I commanded them not."—Jer. vii. 30-31.

"They have built also the high places of Baal, to burn their sons with fire for burnt-offerings unto Baal, which I commanded not."—Jer. xix. 5.

"The Israelites were mingled among the heathen, and learned their works; and they served their idols, which were a snare unto them... For they sacrificed their sons and their daughters unto devils; and shed innocent blood, even the blood of their sons and their daughters, whom they sacrificed unto the idols of Canaan."—Ps. cvi. 35-36-37.

"Moreover, thou hast taken thy sons and thy daughters, whom thou hast borne unto me, and these hast thou sacrificed unto them to be devoured."—Ez. xvi. 20.

"And have also caused their sons, whom they bear unto me, to pass for them through the fire to devour them.... For when they had slain their children to their idols, then they came the same day into My sanctuary to profane it."—Ex. xxiii. 37-39.

"Jephthah vowed to the Lord... and offered up for a burnt-offering, or sacrifice, his own daughter."—Judges xi. 29-40.

4—2

compliment on the integrity of the Roman Catholics in contradistinction to Protestants, who were always in the habit of altering their Bibles whenever it suited their purposes.

In Matthew xii. 40 it was declared that Christ would be in the heart of the earth three days and three nights, but did not the event falsify this prediction? Did Christ remain three days and three nights in the tomb? He died on Friday, and rose on the Sunday; by what extended interpretation could that be made to mean three days and three nights? Even Dr. Claughton had failed to explain this away, when in a recent controversy with a Secularist the latter put him this question, and it was not to be expected that his opponent would be more successful. He knew that his opponent's party would attempt some sort of answer, but they might be sure that he would receive the answer for what it was worth.

It was well known amongst Oriental nations that good omens were invariably the harbingers of propitious events, and that ill omens sufficiently indicated the nature of the events that would follow. He could adduce various instances to prove the truth of this statement from several ancient books, but one would suffice. It was said of the wife of the Emperor Bimbisara that when she had conceived the longing she had was to drink the blood of her husband. When this was satisfied, she gave birth to a prince, who in time killed his father, the Emperor, and obtained the Crown. This shewed that an ill omen prefigured an unpropitious event. And what were the omens about the time of the birth of the being who came to save the world? Why, a massacre of thousands of little innocents. Did not this incident indicate that Christ was a pretender who came to the world with the view of casting men into perdition? Let them, therefore, remember that no salvation in a future state could reasonably be expected by believing in such a being. It was also quite clear that Christ did not rise again, and that his disciples made away with his body at night, as it was feared that they would do. To this part of the subject he would recur on the next day.

Now what were the signs that preceded Buddha's ministry on earth? He would refer to a few of the thirty-two good and cheerful omens and wonders that are mentioned in the books as having appeared on the day that he was conceived of King Sudhodhana in the womb of the Queen Mahamaya, on the day of his birth, and of his attaining Buddahood, namely, receiving the use of eyes, ears, and legs by those who had been blind, deaf, and cripple from their birth, the mitigation of the pains in the several hells, the allaying of the pangs of hunger and thirst of those evil spirits that had been condemned to roam about in the universe, and the curing of all hitherto incurable diseases. Were not these signs sufficient to shew that the object of Buddha's ministry was to bring happiness and true bliss to this world, and to introduce into it a true religion? How unlike were these to those hideous omens relating to Christ's birth, which it was not even possible to mention without a shudder and doing violence to one's kindly feelings. If his opponents are in a position to shew that even an ant had died in consequence of Buddha's birth, he would give them *his* word, —he was not speaking for his *confrères*—that he would renounce Buddhism as speedily as possible. This unusually stirring speech was brought to a close by the Priest in these words :—" Christ is not our authority, neither is Buddha. Weigh without prejudice the arguments that have been adduced on either side: consider which party has failed to answer the questions put to it, and hold fast the faith of the reasonable party. I may have introduced some warmth into the discussion of the subjects: why was that? why have I been so earnest? Simply because I so love the truth and see such an immense multitude, to whom I have to offer my best thanks for their patient attention."

CONTINUATION OF THE BUDDHIST CONTRO-
VERSY AT PANTURA.

THE REV. F. S. SIRIMANNE'S SPEECH.

During the preceding day, Wednesday, it having been
decided at a meeting held by the several clergymen assembled
in Pantura, that a more fluent speaker, and one whose
language "will be understanded of the common people,'
should address the multitude, the task of opening the
proceedings of the second or the last day fell on Mr F S.
Sirimanne, a catechist of the Church Missionary Society. as
he was considered, next to Rev. C. Jayesinghe, who is not at
all controversially inclined, the best popular speaker in the
Singhalese ranks of the Christians. Unknown to the other
intelligent natives of this Island, this follower of the Church
Missionaries has, since the termination of his connection with
the Buddhist priests of Galpata wihare, been working in
comparative seclusion amongst the lower classes of Colombo,
holding forth against Buddhism and expounding the Bible
doctrine of salvation to the hundreds who flock around to
hear the loud stentorian tones of this bland speaker, whenever
he addresses them at the different places appointed for "open
air" preaching.

Mr. Sirimanne commenced by stating that in the same
manner as fever patients had a dislike for food be it ever so
wholesome, the Priest, who was suffering with the fever of
ignorance, could not appreciate the value of the precious
doctrines of the Bible; and had raised several objections
against Christianity because the truth appeared to him false.
But he would assure them that not a single argument had
been adduced against this pure religion that could not be

met by a boy attending any Christian school. However, as he was addressing a number of persons who were totally unacquainted with Christianity, he would try and answer the Priest as fully as he possibly could within the hour in which he had to speak. But before proceeding further, he had to make a few remarks in regard to the replies given by the Priest to the objections the Christian party had raised against Buddhism. They (the Christians) had stated that Buddha had distinctly denied the existence of a soul, and quoted the words that Gautama had made use of when speaking on this subject, namely, that man had no soul, that nothing remained after death, and that nothing went to another state of existence. But what were the replies of the rev. Priest to this? These only served the purpose of confirming their objections, and proving plainly that there was a soul. Buddhists command the performance of meritorious actions, but how did these avail if there were no soul that goes to another world? The Priest also asked them to state the nature of the soul, the existence of which the Christians did not deny. The soul is an immaterial and invisible substance and has no form; therefore to ask its form to be shewn is to require that which was not possible. Has the Priest forgotten that according to Buddhism even that such invisible and unnatural beings exist, and that *Arupa Brahma loka* is said to be wholly peopled with such spirits. If the whole of what constituted man perished here and there were no *Atma* that proceeded to another world, there would be no necessity for a religion, and it was because there was such a state of existence hereafter that they required to believe on the true God, with the view of attaining eternal happiness.

And now with reference to the arguments raised against the holy Christian religion by the Priest. Because God was called a 'ealous God in the Bible, it did not follow that he was envious: he was a perfectly holy and righteous being. The word "'ealous" as applied to God in the Bible only signified that he will not give his glory to another person or thing. A great deal was also made, by the Priest, of God's command to Moses to perform certain miracles before Pharaoh, and if these had not the desired effect of letting the children of Israel go, to perform others; such orders were given simply because Pharaoh was exceedingly haughty and questioned who Jehovah was, when Moses first took his message to the King of Egypt: God then assured Moses that he would take out his people with a mighty hand with the view of shewing both Pharaoh and the Israelites who he was. Till the infliction of the tenth plague, God well knew what the effect of each previous plague would be, but he ordered Moses to work these different miracles and send the various plagues to shew his might to Pharaoh, and to all succeeding generations. That God was not ignorant of Pharaoh's purposes is clear from Exod. iii. 19, wherein it is said, "And I am sure that the King of Eygpt will not let you go, no, not by a mighty hand."

To prove that God was fond of human blood, allusion had also been made by the Priest to the circumcision of Moses' son by Zipporah, but the Priest has, either through ignorance or deliberately, distorted facts. Zipporah did not, as was alleged, cast the foreskin of her son at God's feet, but at Moses'. Her exclamation, "Surely a bloody husband art thou to me," clearly shews this, even if the use of the non-honorific third personal pronoun in speaking of the person at whose feet the skin was thrown in the Singhalese Bible did not remove all doubt on this point.

With reference to the incident mentioned in Judges i. 19, that the Lord could not drive out the inhabitants of the valley because they had chariots of iron, the Priest made out the reason of this to be that Jehovah feared iron chariots. But it was not so, for did not the Lord subdue a host of 900 iron chariots only very shortly after; and completely destroy Pharaoh and his iron chariots when the children of Israel were brought out of Egypt? it was not because the Lord feared iron chariots that Judah did not meet with success in this instance, but simply because he lacked faith in God. He was able to defeat the enemy only when he trusted in God; but no sooner did he lose faith and fear iron chariots, than he was discomfited. All the events mentioned in the Bible, besides being historically true, were so ordered by the omniscient God with the view of revealing spiritual lessons to future generations; and this incident was recorded in order to prove the power and importance of faith.

In attempting to compare the Buddhist doctrine of the eternity of man with the Bible account of the creation, the Priest, with the view of misleading the ignorant, had stated some ridiculous absurdities. His argument was that because God breathed into Adam's nostrils the breath of life, therefore it was a portion of God's soul that was thus breathed; and as God was everlasting, that man, who only became a living soul after this infusion of the breath of life, was also without beginning or end. What a ridiculous inference! The passage referred to only meant that God gave life to man and deposited the soul in him. There was nothing at all there to shew that God parted with a portion of his own soul. What man there present would attach the meaning sought to be put upon this verse by the Priest to the homely Singhalee words, " blow some oil into his ear?" Who will assoiate the idea of blowing a portion of one's living principle with this injunction to infuse a little oil into another's ear? The meaning of the expression in the Bible, " breathing into his nostrils the breath of life," was also the same.

Now as regards the sacrifice of Jephthah's daughter, this is a subject that has been frequently brought forward by the rev. Priest, and on every occasion the reply that she was not killed and sacrificed was given; and yet the Priest does not seem to be satisfied. But supposing even that she had been sacrificed, no blame attaches to God, because he was no party to Jephthah's rash vow. Human sacrifices were explicitly prohibited in the Holy Scriptures; and provision was made in the Jewish code to meet the case of a person making such a rash vow, which was to pay a sum of money as a ransom, and thus save the life of the fellow being. It is nowhere stated in the Bible that Jephtah's daughter was killed, but what appeared there was that she bewailed two months for her virginity, not for her death. And it was also said that her father did unto her according to his vow, and she knew no man, and that the daughters of Israel went yearly to lament the daughter of Jephthah, four days in a year. This ceremony was gone through two months before the accomplishment of the vow and was periodically repeated. So it is quite clear that from that day she only lived a virgin ; and therefore to say that Jephthah's daughter was sacrificed by cutting off her neck was a falsehood.

Another argument raised by the Priest against Christianity was that Christ's prediction that he would be in the heart of the earth three days and three nights was falsified by his having remained in the grave only from Friday till Sunday morning. But anyone acquainted with the Jewish modes of calculation will see that there is no discrepancy at all between the prediction and its fulfilment. The phrase "three days and three nights" was used by the Jews to denote what is generally understood as three days. It was so used in Gen. vii. 12, where it is said that "the rain was upon the earth forty days and forty nights:" which was the same as the expression in 17 v. that the flood was forty days upon the earth. In the same manner, if it had been said that Christ remained in the heart of the earth three days, which is the same, according to Jewish idiom, as saying three days and three nights, there would have been no difficulty at all, for surely the Priest will not deny that Christ remained in the grave on Friday, Saturday, and Sunday. True, he was not in the tomb either the whole of Friday or Sunday, but according to Jewish phraseology any portion of a day was spoken of as a whole day, and numerous instances can be cited from ancient writers in support of such an usage. And so much for the vaunted objection which was alleged to have been adduced by an able European, and with which the Priest intended to make short work of Christianity.

In order to shew that Christ's birth was anything but beneficial to mankind, the Priest mentioned the massacre of the innocents as an ill omen, which indicated that something the reverse of good would result by his birth. The Priest was however mistaken : no ill omen attended the birth of Christ; and it was nowhere said that thousands of children were killed at his birth. The Priest said so either with the view of deceiving those who were present or being ignorant of the facts. Two years after Christ's birth, it was perfectly true that the wicked King

Herod, having heard from the magicians that Christ would become a mighty King, caused many infants of two years old to be massacred, apprehending some danger to his crown; but by this massacre no injury resulted to the infants, because as there is no doubt that their souls went to heaven, it only expedited their enjoyment of eternal bliss; and as for the parents, why it may have been the means of bringing them to repentance, and thereby to everlasting happiness.

These were all the remarks he (the Catechist) had to make in regard to the objections raised against Christianity; but he now saw a very short way of ending this controversy, and would tell his hearers what it was. The rev. Priest had in his last lecture said if it could be shewn that even an ant had been killed at Buddha's birth, that he would renounce Buddhism. He (the Catechist) was in a position to shew that greater beings than ants had been deprived of their lives in consequence of Buddha's birth, and if the Priest were a man of his word he ought at once to renounce Buddhism: then would this controversy be satisfactorily ended, and their object accomplished.

He would now enumerate some of the many instances in which death ensued on account of, or by means of, Buddha, and would beg of the Buddhist portion of his audience particularly to lend him a patient hearing, as they had heard what their champion had said—that he would forsake Buddhism if it could be proved that even an ant had been killed at Buddha's birth. In the first place, Buddha's own mother died seven days after giving birth to this extraordinary baby, who is said to have been able to walk and speak very plainly at the moment of his birth. The wonder is that the mother of such a gigantic monster should have lived even for seven days. Thus they will see that the death of the queen of the highest emperor of India was caused at the instance of Buddha, and was not her death of greater consequence than that of an ant? Secondly, it appears in the sacred books of the Buddhists that men and even beasts died by the roaring of lions: these lions exist even at the present day in the Himalaya Mountains, situated to the north of India, though

we in Ceylon cannot even hear their roaring ; if it were so
and the ancients did die by hearing these poor lions roar, how
many millions of creatures would have perished at hearing
the roaring of the lion Gautama, whose exclamation
" *Ayyo 'ham asmi lokassa jettho ham asmi lokassa settho
'ham asmi lokassa,*" just after his birth, is said to have been
heard by the gods of the uppermost Brahma world. Numerous other instances of the deaths of men and beasts caused on
account of Buddha could be cited, but he thought those he
had just mentioned were sufficient for the present. They
had all heard the construction put upon the so-called good
and evil omens attendant on the birth of Christ and Buddha
by the Priest. He did not agree with it; and before arriving
at any conclusion, he would entreat his hearers to hear the
Christians' interpretation of these signs. Christ came into
the world to destroy the power of sin, and to set up the
kingdom of righteousness. The subjects of the kingdom
of sin opposed the Saviour by bad omens, as this
Priest terms them, and did their best to retain those
sinful pleasures in which they revelled. It was only natural
that this should be so. They could not possibly expect a
different reception, and that was the reason for the so-called
bad omens. But in the case of Buddha it was different.
He was a sinner, as other men were, and came to this world
to encourage vice, and enlarge its kingdom, and no wonder
that this sinful world welcomed him with good omens, just
as drunkards would receive with open arms one of their own
number, but spurn a teetotaller.

And now, with reference to Buddhism Before embracing any religion, it is the duty of each one to examine
whether the books on which that religion rests are au-
thentic or not Buddhism that prevails in this Island
has for its authority only the Three Pitakas, and it
was, therefore, incumbent on them to find out what these
books were, when they were written, and whether they did
contain the doctrines of Buddha as propounded by him ; in
short, whether there is any testimony for their authenticity.
He will tell them, however, that these Pitakas were committed
to writing not in the land where Buddha is said to have lived,

not by those who heard him preach, and not during his life-time, or that of those who were his contemporaries; but, according to *Mahawansa* and *Sarasangraha*, four hundred and fifty years after Buddha's death, at a convocation of priests in Aluwihare of Matella in this very Island. Up to that day Buddha's sayings were transmitted orally, and what weight could be attached, the Catechist imploringly asked of his audience, to such documents, which simply stated that some four or five hundred years ago there lived a sage in a distant land called Dambhadiva, etc.; and he is said to have ex-pounded such and such doctrines? Would a last will, with such meagre evidence, be considered genuine in a Court of Justice? If not, how are they to receive as true documents which concern matters of such great moment as the salvation of men's souls? It is also stated in Buddhist books that Gautama attained Buddahood by the observance of the ten *Paramita* (or sacrifices); and so it will be well to see whether those rites or offerings could have the effect which they are said to have had. The first *Paramita* or observance they read of as having been performed by Buddha with the view of accumulating merit, and attaining the Budda-hood, is *Dana paranita*, or almsgiving, which, besides others, consisted of the extraordinary offering of his eyes, head, flesh, blood, wives and children.

Many of those present knew with what love, care, and attention a daughter is brought up by the parents; how at her proper age, whatever their affection to each other may be, when she is given in marriage to an utter stranger, the attachment to her parents gives place to love for her newly found husband, and how the wife looks solely to her husband for her comfort and sustenance. They were also not unacquainted with the fact that the birth of children only tended to strengthen this bond of union, and form a happy family. And what will they think of a father, living in such happiness, giving up his children without any hesitation or sorrow to a wandering hermit, amidst the cries and lamentations of his wife and the children themselves, without any inquiry as to what he was going to do with them, simply because he came to the door of this happy abode, and said—may be with some base motive of selling them as slaves or otherwise maltreating them—Give me your two children as an alms offering, and you will attain Buddahood? Not satisfied with this, if even the wife be thus sacrificed, what would they think of such a husband? Were these meritorious acts? Was it meritorious to break the hearts of wives and children and bring desolation and misery to a happy home? If it were, what actions will they enumerate under the head of demerits or sins? But yet Gautama did all this, and this was the means he adopted to attain Buddahood. How often did he so give up his wives and children? Was it a hundred times? No! A thousand times? Oh no! As the science of figures cannot sufficiently express the number of wives and children so sacrificed, in order to convey to the mind of the reader an approximate idea of the number offered, it is said in Buddhist works that if the ropes and strings with which the wives and children of Buddha who were sacrificed by him were tied with, were collected into a heap, its height would be a million times greater than that of Mahameru which he (the Catechist) would remind them was 84 000 yoduns high—and 16 miles went to make up one yoduna. This will give them a tolerably good idea of the number of wives and children sacrificed. Did his hearers believe that any happy state could be attained by the commission of such barbarous and cruel actions? There would be an end to all social happiness, and to even the continuance of the world, if everybody set about perpetrating such horrible crimes as those which Buddha is said to have done to attain Buddahood. But these were not all the offerings he made to gain this end. It is said that the number of his eyes he sacrificed was more than the stars of the sky, the quantity of blood he gave was more than the water in the ocean, and the quantity of flesh was greater than the substance of this earth, and that of his heads was more than the height of Mahameru. What a mass of men must have been killed to offer so many eyes, hands and heads! Even if, as is declared, it was Gautama's own eyes and hands which were offered, self-destruction was quite as bad as killing a third person, and so the heinousness of the crime was the same, and what do they think of a being who committed such villainy to attain a state of bliss ?

Buddha is also said to have been omniscient: but they will find from instances he will presently mention that his omniscience was of a peculiar nature, and that it represented dead people as living, and those who were actually living as being dead. For instance, in Mahawage it is said that Buddha, at the commencement of his ministry, did not consider it worth while to preach Bana, as it was his impression that there was not a single being on earth who could understand his doctrines and be edified by them; but shortly after it is stated that he was the means of sending twenty-four Asanka souls to Nirwana. Was it not plain from this that Buddha did not possess any omniscient power. If he had he would not have failed to see even one of these twenty-four Asanka beings who were edified by Buddha discourses. Then again after Maha Brahma convinced Gautama of the falsity of this idea he cherished, that there was no human being on earth competent enough to understand his doctrines, he decided on preaching his *Dhamma* to Alarakalama as being the most intelligent man alive. But did he carry out his wishes? No; the All-wise Buddha found on inquiry that Alarakalama had been dead some days, and there was no possibility of preaching to him. His second choice then fell on Uddukarama, but the object of this selection also shared the same fate. On making inquiry for this sage, he found that he too had been dead some time. If they believed this helpless being, who committed so many and terrible mistakes, and who often had to be corrected by third parties, to be all-wise, who would not be omniscient? Lastly, Buddhists pray to, or take refuge in, Buddha, Dharma,—that is in his doctrines contained in the Three Pitakas—and in the priesthood, in the words which his Buddhist friends often repeat:—

Buddhan saranam gaccami,
Dhamman saranam gaccami,
Sangham saranam gaccami.

But what was the use in taking refuge, or *sarana*, in either of these? Was there any protection to be gained by it?

In the first place, as there is no sun-light when there is no sun, so they could not expect any protection from a being who was non-existent. Buddha is said to have attained the state of annihilation, and how could he become any refuge? It was plain, therefore, that this first *sarana*, or refuge, was of no avail. The second—the refuge in Dhamma or Bana books—was no better; how could a man take refuge in books? It is rather that the books are under the care and protection of men, who get them transcribed into olas, and keep them bound up safely in an almirah, or chest, to prevent their being destroyed. Was it not clear that this refuge, or *sarana*, too was of no avail? And as regards the third *sarana*—or the refuge in priests—he need not say much. Between the two sects of the Buddhist priesthood—the Amerapura and Siam—a controversy has been raging for some time, each trying to prove that the other has no *Upasampada*, ordination, *sarana*, or Sila, or many other observances—in short, that they were no priests. First, then, they had to decide as to whether they *were* priests, about which even amongst themselves there were such great disputes; and even if they could come to a decision, what availed it? The immorality of the priests was well known; and was it not like the blind leading the blind for the Buddhist priests, men full of lust, envy, and ignorance as they were, to attempt to guide the people who foolishly took refuge in the *Sangha*, or the priesthood? Now in conclusion, he would remind his auditory that not a word had been said by the reverend priest to explain the confusing and absurd doctrine of *Patic-casamuppada*, nor as to the Buddhist *Atma*, and would entreat of them to consider, without prejudice, all that he said, seek the truth so that it may be found, and after proving all things, hold fast that which was good.

THE BUDDHIST'S REPLY.

THE REV. MIGETTUWATTE'S THIRD SPEECH.

The Priest Migettuwatte, here rising, said that he had invited the several learned priests there present to the controversy, believing that some able opponent would appear on the Christian side, and that *their* assistance would be required to refute the arguments that might be adduced, but having been surprisingly disappointed in this, he did not think it necessary to give his friends further trouble by detaining them longer. Before, however, making any comments on the lecture of his friend the Catechist, he would say a few words in regard to some remarks that fell from his opponent on a previous occasion. He (the Rev. Silva) stated that Buddhism was not worthy of credence as it likened man unto a frog, serpent, or a dog. By making this assertion his opponent not only damaged his own cause, but betrayed his ignorance of the Christian Bible, of which he professed to be a preacher. For on turning to Ecclesiastes iii. 19, they would find it stated, " For that which befalleth the sons of men befalleth beasts, even one thing befalleth them, as the one dieth so dieth the other, yea they have all one breath ; so that a man hath no pre-eminence above a beast : for all is vanity." And now he would like to know where in Buddhist scriptures a single passage occurred likening man unto a *beast*.

His opponent, in arguing that Buddhism was not a proper religion to embrace because human beings were likened unto beasts, was only arguing against Christianity, and he was thankful for the assistance from this unexpected quarter. He must say, however, that he was sure this ignorance of the Bible would have cost him his place if the Principal of the Society to which his opponent belonged had been present on the occasion. And if the ignorance of his opponent was so great in matters pertaining to his own religion, the audience would be able to form an idea of the extent of his knowledge of Buddhism, against which he would take this opportunity of mentioning that not a *single* tenable argument had been raised by his opponent.

An attempt was made by him on the previous Tuesday to depreciate Buddhism, by declaring that the doctrine of *Paticcasamuppada* was an absurdity and a confusion of thought. He would now, as promised on that day, try to make this subject a little clearer. Even the sage Buddhaghosa was so conscious of the difficulty of rightly explaining this abstruse doctrine that he expressed himself thus in his work *Visuddhimarga* :—

> *Vattu kamo aham ajja*
> *Paccayakara, vannanam*
> *Patittham na adhigaccami*
> *Ajjagutho na sagaran* :—

the literal meaning of which is, "that as there is no support to one who has fallen into the ocean, I who am fallen into the sea of *Paticcasamuppada* doctrine have no support;" but the idea sought to be conveyed by this stanza is that it was only those wise men who have attained the *arihat* that were able to fully comprehend this theory, and that others, not so fortunate, could not easily understand it. And the attempt made by his opponent, who professed to fully understand it, to carp at *Paticcasamuppada*, of which even the great and learned commentator, well-versed in the Three Pitakas, spoke in such terms as those he had above quoted, can only be compared to the barking of a dog envious at the splendour of the moon. That his opponent had not the remotest idea of this doctrine of causation was plainly shewn by the example of the father begetting the son, and the son begetting the father he adduced in illustration of it. True, there was an instance of such a circumlocutory genesis in the Christian Scriptures which he would advert to on a future occasion. He would now, however, endeavour to explain to the best of his ability what this doctrine of *Paticcasamuppada* is, and would beg of the multitude to give him an attentive hearing.

The doctrine of *causation* is enunciated in the following passage :—*Avijja paccaya samkhara, samkhara paccaya vinnanam, vinnana paccaya nama rupam, nama rupa paccaya salayatanam, salayatana paccaya phasso, phassa paccaya vedana, vedana paccaya tanha, tanha paccaya upadanam, upadana paccaya bhavo, bhava paccaya jati, jati paccaya jaramaranam soka, paridera dukkha domanass upayasa sambharanti.*

The gist of which is that in consequence of, or from

avijja, samkharas are produced, in consequence of, or from
samkharas, vinana is produced, in consequence of, or from
vinnana, nama rupa is produced, etc. In short, what Buddha
evidently meant to say was that in regular succession all
these are produced causatively one from the other, but this of
course his opponent could' not understand, which was the
reason for his stating the ridiculous nonsense they heard,
that *samkhara* was produced from a thing called *avijja* which
existed independent of a sentient being, and that *vinnana*
was produced from *samkhara*. To shew the incorrectness of
his opponent's views, and the further elucidation of this
subject, he would give them a short example. Though,
when it is said curd is made *of* milk, butter *from* curd, and
ghee *from* butter, and each of these is different from the
other, yet there can be no possible doubt that all these, curd,
milk, butter and ghee, existed together. In like manner,
there never existed *avijja* alone without a sentient being, n...
samkhara alone, independent of, or without *avijja*, nor the
two *nama rupa* by themselves, independent of, or without
samkhara. That all these exist together is certain.* And
there was no doubt that his opponent put a different construction altogether on the words that Buddha uttered to
shew the manner of the transmigratory movements of a
sentient being through *Samsara* or metempsychosis. All his
opponent's utterances on this subject reminded him of the
babbling of a madman. The *Patthanapprakarana* of *Ab-
hidarma* also has the following in regard to the doctrine of
Paticcasamuppada :—

*Moham paticcasampayuttaka khanda patisandhikkhane pat-
tum patticca sahetuka khandhanam, etc.*

And it signifies that the *skhandhas* connected with the
ignorance (*i.e.,* of the present existence) and *skhandhas* connected with the form of the object (which he sees at the
point of death) are born.

---

* The most learned Buddhist with whom I conversed in the East
denied utterly the existence of matter. It was only an appearance, a
shadow. The only two realities in the universe were causation and
spiritual substance.

In order to shew that *samkharas* never come to existence alone, the work entitled *Visudhimarga* says thus :—

Samkhara kamma paccayena ca upanissaya paccayena ca paccaya honti, etc.

That is, *samkharas* become sources of *vinnana* from the source of *kamma* (or deed), or from source and association.

The following passage will also shew that *vinnana* does not come into existence before *nama rupa*, but simultaneously with them :—

Vipaka vinnana sahajati anna manna nissaya sampayutta vipaka ahara indriya atthi avigata paccaychi navadha paccaya honti.

The purport of this is that the productive *vinnana* is produced from nine different sources of coeval birth, mutual, causal, associating, joined to each other, productive, objective, existing in perception and separated. If one thus understands and can comprehend this abstruse doctrine aright, it will be impossible for him to come to the conclusion that *nama rupa* came into existence after *vinnana*, and the endeavour of his opponent, with such a limited knowledge, to fathom this mysterious doctrine of *Paticcasamuppada* was like the roaming of a blind elephant in a thick jungle. He would here remind those present that no explanation had been given by his opponent of what his party understood by *Atma*, if it was not the cleaving to existence of which he had already spoken. He would again impress on them that the being who according to them (the Buddhists) suffered hereafter was not a different one. Each continued his individuality. All knew themselves in the future life. Why the Christians put the construction that they did on the Buddhist doctrine, viz., that it was a *different being* that suffered in a future state for actions committed in this life. was owing to their incapability to understand this subject properly.

And now before proceeding to meet the objections of hi1 friend the Catechist, he would make another remark in reference to Christianity. In I. Corinthians xv. 22-28, it was said, "For as in Adam all die, even so in Christ shall all be made alive"—which statement clearly shewed—and it is the belief of these Christians—that by believing on Christ every one shall escape the punishment of eternal hell-fire and obtain everlasting happiness. But there was another passage in the Bible which had quite a different meaning, and he would like to know how the Christians reconciled two such diametrically contradictory declarations. He referred to Matt. xxv. 41-46, wherein appeared the words—"Then shall he say also unto them on the left hand, Depart from me, ye cursed, into everlasting fire prepared for the devil and his angels: For I was an hungered, and ye gave me no meat. I was thirsty, and ye gave me no drink: I was a stranger, and ye took me not in; naked, and ye clothed me not; sick and in prison, and ye visited me not. Then shall they also answer him saying, Lord, when saw we thee an hungered, or athirst, or a stranger, or in prison, and did not minister to thee? Then shall he answer them saying, Verily I say unto you, inasmuch as ye did it not to one of the least of these, ye did it not to me. And these shall go away into everlasting punishment; but the righteous unto life eternal." If words have any meaning, this clearly shews that men's salvation does not depend upon belief in Christ alone; but to attain happiness hereafter it was necessary to perform righteous or good actions. Then what did Christians mean by declaring that *all* who believe on Christ's name would be saved? If one portion of the Bible so hopelessly contradicts another portion, which *one* were they to accept as true? It was certain that both statements could not be true, and which was the false one? What right had they then to believe in a Bible which contained so many contradictions? and were they not justified in coming to the conclusion that a religion based upon such a *book*, was false? *

---

* Among discrepancies, contradictions, and irreconcilable passages in the Bible, the following were selected by the Rev. M. Wollaston, an English clergyman, of Melbourne, Australia :—

Now with refcrence to the remarks made by his friend, the Catechist. A more desultory and unscholar-like speech he had never heard, and it would be usele·s to even touch on those parts of his discourse which were quite irrelevant to the issue, as the curing of a fever patient, etc. It had been said by the Catechist that the Buddhist party had only confirmed the objections raised against *Pancaskhandha* by the Christians, but this was totally untrue; they had completely refuted all arguments raised against this abstruse doctrine by

---

2nd Sam., xxiv. v. 1.—"Ard *the Lord* moved David" to number the children of Israel.

9.—"Joab gave up the number of the people unto the king, and there were in Israel, 800,000 men that drew the sword, aud the men of Judah were 500,000 men!" or a total of 1,300,000.

13.—" So Gad came to David and said unto him, Shall *seven* years of famine come unto thee in thy land?" etc.

24.—" So David bought the threshing-floor and the oxen for *fifty* shekels of *silver;*" equal to £5 of our money, at two shillings the shekel.

For I have seen God face to face. —Gen. xxxii. 30.

And they saw the God of Israel. —Ex. xxiv. 19.

He rested and was refreshed.— Ex. xxi. 19.

I am weary with repenting.—Jer. xv. 6.

The eyes of the Lord are in every place.—Prov. xv. 3.

Is there anything too hard for me?—Jer. xxxi 27.

With God all things are possible. —Mat·. xix. 26.

God is not a man * * that he should repent.—Num. xxiii. 19.

Those that seek me early shall find me.—Prov. viii. 17.

To undo the heavy burdens, and to let the oppressed go free, and that ye break every yoke.—Is. lviii. 6.

I. Chron., xxi. v. 1.—', And *Satan* stood up, and provoked David to number Israel."

5.—" And Joab gave the sum of the number of the people to David. And all they of Israel were 1,100.000 men that drew the sword; and Judah was 470,000 men that drew the sword," or a total of 1,570,000.

11.—" So Gad came to David and said unto him. Choose thee either *three* years of famine," etc.

25.—" So David gave to Ornan for the place, *six hundred* shekels of *gold*," equal to £1.050 of our money, at £1 15s. per shekel.

No man hath seen God at any time.—John i. 18.

Whom no man hath seen nor can see.—I. Tim. vi. 16.

The Creator * * fainteth not, neither is weary.—Is. xl. 28.

And the Lord came down to see the city and the tower.—G·n. xi. 5.

And the Lord was with Judah * * but could not drive out the inhabitants of the valley, because they had chariots of iron.—Judges i. 19.

And God repented of the evil he had said.—Jonah iii. 10.

They shall seek me early, but shall not find me.—Prov. i. 28.

Of the children of the strangers that do sojourn among you, of them shall ye buy. * * They shall be your bondmen for ever.—Lev. xxv. 45, 46.

the Christians, and th's all those who were present would remember. He (the Priest) had never denied the exis'ence of a future state, but what he required was simply that the opposite party should explain to him the nature of what they meant by *Atma*. He had most plainly shewn them what they (the Buddhists) understood by the idea of cleaving to existence which took shape at death. The Catechist mentioned something about the dwellers of the *Arupa Brahma loka* in explanation of *Atma*, but if his friend had correctly understood what was said in regard to *Arupa Brahma loka*, he was sure he would not have brought it forward as an illustration.

S:me nonsense was also uttered by the Catechist in reply to the remarks made by him (the Priest), with reference to God's command to Moses to perform a series of miracles before Pharaoh, according to the effect that each one produced, thereby shewing that God was not omniscient; to meet this objection his friend declared that the plagues had been inflicted on Egypt to punish Pharaoh for his haughtiness; but what had that to do with the command "do this and if that won't induce him to let the people go, do the other, etc." Those of the assembly who had any common sense would be able to judge of the inappropriateness of this reply to the objection he raised.

The reply his friend made to his remarks on the circumcision of Moses' son was not more happy. It was plainly declared in the Bible that when Zipporah, Moses' wife, knew that God was angry with Moses and so' 'it to kill him, she circumcised their son and cast the foreskin at his feet, and this was instanced by him to shew the fondness of the Christians' God for human blood as a sacrifice, in common with devils and other evil spirits; the course adopted to appease whom, he would again remind them, was the *same* as that pursued by Zipporah in the passage he had just cited. The Catechist could not have possibly understood his (the Priest's) meaning; if he did he would not certainly have adduced such a ridiculous reply as he had done. He contented himself by saying that the foreskin was cast at Moses' feet. Apart from the absurdity of endeavouring to convince them that the sacrifice with which *God's* wrath was sought tc be appeased was thrown at *Moses'* feet!—what a feeble reply it was to his remark that God was fond of human sacrifices. It was God that sought to kill Moses and yet his friend declares that the bloody offering was thrown at Moses' feet. How absurd!

The incident with reference to the armies of Judah fleeing from iron chariots, though the Lord was with them, was also mentioned by him (the Priest) to shew that, like other evil spirits, the Jewish God feared iron. If he did not fear iron, why was not Judah, with whom the Lord was, more successful? The Catechist, in his reply, declared that the discomfiture of the armies of Judah was not owing to any fear of iron, but for lack of Judah's faith. If then Judah had no faith, why did the Christians' God, whom they declared to be omniscient, abide with him? When he joined him, if he were omniscient, he would have known that Judah did not possess faith; and would have foreseen these disastrous consequences; and yet he remains with him till the last, and only flees when the iron chariots appeared! Did not this clearly shew that either God was not omniscient or that he feared iron? How will his friend get out of this dilemma? He would here warn him (the Catechist) not to venture on such answers in future, which precipitated him into new difficulties.

To shew that Jehovah did not breathe a portion of his own soul into Adam (which was the inference to be drawn from the passage, "The Lord God formed man of the dust of the ground, and breathed into his nostrils the breath of life, and man became a living soul"), his friend instanced the case of blowing oil into a man's ear, and asked whether that ever meant blowing a portion of a man's life with the oil. What silly talk was this! In saying that oil was blown into one's ear would it be inferred that "the breath of life was blown into him?"—which was the expression made use of in the passage, and which, therefore, warranted his saying that it was a portion of the spirit of God that was breathed, or infused, into **Adam**.

The Catechist also attempted to shew that Jephthah's daughter was not killed and sacrificed, by stating that she was ransomed by paying a certain sum of money to Jehovah, but it was distinctly said in the Bible that Jephthah *did* unto her according to his vow, which was, they will remember, to offer up unto the Lord as a burnt offering whatever came forth of the doors of his house to meet him when he returns in peace from the children of Ammon. Well, what was the doing unto her according to his vow if it were not offering his daughter, who came to meet him, as a burnt offering to Jehovah? If they were not satisfied with this, there was the Douay Bible, which he would be happy to hand to his opponents for their delectation, which would conclusively shew that the neck of Jephthah's daughter was really cut off, and offered to Jehovah. He (the Priest) regretted very much that he was under the necessity of engaging in controversies with those who ev n attempted to deny facts, which were supported by such incontrovertible testimony.

With reference to his statement that on account of Christ's birth several helpless innocents had been killed, the Catechist had the audacity to declare that he (the Priest) said that the innocents were slain at Christ's birth, or on the day of his birth, and proceeded to demolish that imaginary objection. He never mentioned that the innocents were killed at Christ's birth, but only that, on account of Christ's birth, many had been killed by Herod. If the Catechist had any regard for *truth*, he would not have uttered such a *falsehood* before an assembly of the kind before him, and who would remember what he actually said. Being unable to deny this whole-sale massacre of little children on account of the coming of Christ, the Catechist sought to cast obloquy of a similar kind on Buddha, by alleging that Buddha's mother died seven days after his birth. But the death of Buddha's mother, however, was not in consequence of Buddha's birth. It is clearly seen from Buddhist books that before a Bhodisat (or Buddha) leaves the abode of the gods to be born in this world he foresees five things, one of these five being the duration of his mother's life; and in this instance it appears that he was incarnated in his mother's womb just ten months and seven days before the day on which he foresaw she would terminate her existence on earth. He was born in ten months, and as pre-ordained she died at the expiration of the remaining seven days. How unreasonable then was it to attribute to Buddha the death of his mother, who had only paid her debt to nature at the appointed time. How could a controversy be carried on with a party who misrepresented the statements so clearly made in Buddhist scriptures? No misrepresentation nor concealment of facts, however, would help them to give a fairer complexion to the slaying of helpless innocents on account of Christ's birth, than the circumstance actually bears and which he explained to them on a previous occasion. To clear Christ from the imputation that he was to be blamed for this act, the Catechist declared that Christ was an enemy of sin, and that therefore the omen of the sinful massacring of innocents was presented at his birth. This answer, however, was extremely stupid. The appearance of sinful signs would indicate that he was rather a *friend* than an *enemy* of sin. At the birth of one who is to bring happiness to this world, a good omen must present itself, and as the slaughter of children was not a good sign, there was no doubt that it only portended the introduction of a false religion on earth and consequent evil to man.

The truth or otherwise of omens is one that can be experienced by anyone, for even the success of a journey is often prefigured by the omens that shew themselves at starting. It was not necessary, however, to enlarge on this subject as he had fully treated of it before. The only advantage which the Catechist derived by *this*, his explanation of the omens, was that the audience were enabled to form a correct opinion of his intelligence. But even this did not betray his friend's stupidity and ignorance so much as did the construction he had put upon the beautiful simile used in Buddhist books to convey an idea of the power and excellence of Buddha's speech. The expression made use of in the books is that at Gautama's birth he made an *abhita kesara sinha nadaya*, which his friend interpreted literally as the roaring of an undaunted lion of the kesara or maned kind, and declared that owing to this roaring of Buddha, which rent the ears of all creatures, several animals had died. It would be impossible for the intelligent portion of his audience to repress their laughter at this silly and stupid explanation, and as Buddhism could not in any way suffer from such feeble attacks, they could well afford to treat it with contempt. According to his friend's interpretation Rajasingha signified a "lion king," instead of a valiant king, which was its proper meaning. Would his friend, however, be good enough to cite a single authority for his statement that anyone suffered any injury at this "lion-like" roaring of Buddha.

His friend also declared that the *Tripitaka*, which comprises all Buddhist doctrines, were only consigned to writing 450 years after Buddha's death, and that, as up to that time, his teachings were transmitted orally, the doctrines must have been put in writing according to the fancy of the priests who lived at the time, who it was not to be supposed would be able to retain correctly in their memories *all* they had heard. This, however, was all untrue! It was certain that fifty-three years after Buddha's attaining Nirvana, during the reign of Walagambahu, that the preaching of Buddha was consigned to writing in this Island, and even during Buddha's lifetime it is recorded that Buddha's sermons were engraved on *gold leaves*. The authenticity of our Sacred Books cannot be doubted by any truly learned man!

In this Island the Buddhist scriptures were written by Rahats, who were holy and sinless beings, possessed of celestial knowledge, devoid of all passions, and only inferior to Buddha, and hence had no difficulty whatever in retaining anything in their memory for any length of time and correctly consigning *all* they had heard to writing, without adding to, or detracting one *iota* from what Buddha really uttered. The case of the Christian Bible was, however, different. It was not written by such holy personages as those whom he had just mentioned, but by sinful and despicable men, such as Moses, who had committed murders and fled the country. Besides, it was recorded that the Bible thus written was once completely burnt, but that one of Jehovah's Kapuralas (devil's priest) re-wrote it, evidently as suited his purposes, and somehow managed to impose it upon the king as a genuine work.

Speaking of Moses, he could not but mention what occurred to him in regard to the miracles he is said to have performed in Egypt. It was said that the magicians of Egypt performed the miracles that Moses did. It was his opinion that Moses also was a magician, and to say, then, that the power of Almighty God was with him was absurd! If it were so, the magicians too, must have had this divine power.

The Catechist also made some remarks in regard to the offerings made by Gautama to attain Buddahood, and in particular made mention of his offering his children, as King Wessantara, to a hermit named Jutaka Bamuna; but the Catechist evidently said this, forgetting that before attaining Buddahood, the most supreme state in the universe, it was essential for the aspirant to *conquer all passions*, and particularly the love of worldly possessions; and if, when he was asked to sacrifice his wife and children, King Wessantara, who was in hopes of• becoming Buddha, had refused to do so, it would have shewn him unfit for this high mission on account of his desire to possess wives and children, and therefore it was that King Wessantara offered his children. Besides aged women who have heard the story of King Wessantara and his offerings will remember that no evil befell his children, but happiness was the result of their being given away.

And again, the queen of King Wessantara was not, as alleged by the Catechist, given away to be another man's wife. The fact was that Sakkra, the celestial king of the two god worlds, in order to enable King Wessantara to accomplish his *dana paramita* (the offerings) necessary to attain Buddahood in the highest degree, assumed a human form and presenting himself before King Wessantara obtained his queen as an offering and immediately returned her to the king. Thus the king's last sacrifice was made. It was therefore untrue to say that Buddha gave away his wives to other men in the sense that the Catechist used the expression.

The Catechist's remarks touching the height of the strings with which Buddha's wives were tied if collected into a heap, and so on, were all to no purpose, as these figures were simply made use of in the books to express the number and the self-denying nature of the offerings made by Buddha. Symbols and figures were the methods of speech in Buddha's time. Of course it was not to be expected that his friend (the Catechist) would understand the pleonasm.

With reference to the reply made by the Catechist to his (the Priest's) remarks touching Christ not remaining three days and three nights in the grave, as was declared in the Scriptures, he could only ejaculate *novasanavan* (miserable). The Catechist said that the expression in the Bible "three days and three nights" was meant for three days. Even supposing it were so, Christ having risen on Saturday night, or according to the Catechist's interpretation, before Sunday commenced, he only remained two days in the grave, the Friday and the Saturday, and how can that be made to signify three days and three nights? It was needless for him to say anything more touching the Catechist's feeble remarks. As the hour allotted to him was nearly over, he would now conclude, promising to still more completely prove the falsity of Christianity during the last hour of the controversy. He had not yet shewn the comparative excellence of Jehovah, Christ, and Buddha; this he would thoroughly do in the afternoon. Meanwhile, he would beg of the multitude to keep in mind what had been said and sift the truth from falsehood. Heartily thanking the assembly for the great order which prevailed among them, the Priest brought his discourse to a close.

THE DISCUSSION CONTINUED.

REV. MR. SILVA'S THIRD SPEECH.

Rev. Mr. de Silva rose, and said that as that was the last speech he had to make in that discussion, he asked the assembly to pay due attention.

Referring to the Priest's charge against him for using the term *wiruddha karaya*, opponent, he said that the term was not an improper one for an opponent. He then quoted the following gatha (stanza), and shewed that the word was unobjectionable.

Apannakam thanam eke dutiya ahut akkika eladannaya medhavi tam ganheyyad apannakam. Here the words *apannakam thanam* are translated in the jatakas *aviruddhakaranayak;* the word *virruddha*, therefore, meant a subject about which there was a difference of opinion. *Viruddhakaraya* was, therefore, neither offensive nor improper.

The passage from Eccl. iii. 19, quoted by the opponent to shew that the Bible taught that man was only a bea t is refuted by Eccl. iii. 7. In the former, animal life and the mortality of the body are only meant; but the latter shewed that there was a spirit besides, which went to God who gave it.

The opponent said that *Buddhaghosa*, attempting to explain *Paticcasamuppada*, found himself in unsurmountable difficulty, as one who fell into the deep ocean; but the opponent promises to explain it. Is he more competent than *Buddhaghosa*? Mr. de Silva next reviewed the *Paticcasamuppadaya*, and shewed its absurdity, as in his second speech.

The opponent, explaining the *Catussatya*, appealed to the people, and asked whether *jati*, birth, was not sorrow. But Buddha said : *Pubbe ananussutesu dhammesu cakkhum udapadi nanam udapadi panna udapadi vijja udapadi aloko udapadi;* viz., for the attainment of these previously unknown doctrines, the eye, the knowledge, the wisdom, the clear perception, the lights were developed within me (Buddha). What every man was expected to know, Buddha only knew after he had attained to Buddahood.

Respecting the opponent's objection to men being in heaven if the present soul went there, Mr. Silva said human souls were human souls even in heaven. Men on earth were subject to decay and death; but in heaven they were glorious immortal beings.

Next, the absurdity of the opponent quoting I. Cor. xv. 22, to shew that it contradicted the passages in Matt. xxv. 41-47 and Matt. vii. 13-14, were shewn. In the first passage the opponent confounded the meaning of the words *jivat-wanulabanawaeta*, made alive, with *galavanulabanawaeta*, being saved. Being made alive and being saved are different things. All were made alive through Christ; but from John v. 28 and 29 it would appear that "all that are in the graves shall hear his voice, and shall come forth; they that have done good into the resurrection of life, and they that have done evil into the resurrection of damnation." The opponent evidently did not know the meaning of even the Singhalese words *jivatvanulabanawa* and *galawanulabanawa*. Hence the confusion.

The opponent said that the arupa worlds and their inhabitants were subjects very abstruse, and not easy to explain; but wished to know whether the *Atma*, the soul, was like an egg or a ball. How absurd a question!

The opponent said that even at the time of Buddha the *Dharma* was written on leaves of gold; but the books said *Satthakatham sabbam Buddha vacanam tathagatassa parinibba-nato yava panasadhikani cattari vassa satani tava mati sampanna bhikkhu mukha pathena anesum*; that is, Buddha's words, with the comments, were brought down orally by intelligent priests during 450 years after Buddha's death.

The opponent objected to Moses and his writings because he (Moses) at one time killed an Egyptian. Moses certainly did save the life of an innocent Hebrew by killing an Egyptian, who was going to kill the Hebrew. Moses' act was perfectly justifiable and laudable. Even if it were otherwise, if he were a culprit, he was so before he was called of God. There was nothing to prevent him from obeying God, repenting, and being reformed. Besides, the Christians did not take refuge in Moses. But see the character of some of those in whom the Buddhists take refuge. *Angulimala*, the finger-chained, was a robber and a murderer who killed 999 human beings. He was at once ordained by Buddha and attained, it is said, rahatship. The Buddhists take refuge in him. *Angulimala pirita* is recited by the Buddhists at the present time for protection. *Harantika* was also a robber. He also attained rahatship. The Buddhists take refuge in him. The Demon

Aloka for twelve years consecutively murdered and ate a human being every day. He is said to have attained *sowan.* The Buddhists take refuge in him. Having these things before our opponent, how ridiculous was it to charge Moses of murder, and blaspheme God for calling him to his service.

The opponent denied that Bodhisat ever gave away his wife and children for improper uses. The opponent was either ignorant or cared not to utter falsehood even before such an assembly. In *Kudugotsangi* it is stated that Buddha's wife Yasodhara, taking leave of him to enter nibbanam, addressing Buddha himself, said :—

Neka koti sahassani gocaratthaya dayi mam na tattha rimana homi tuyh atthaya maha mune—Great sage, many thousands of *koti* times thou gavest me away as prey to lions, etc., yet I was not displeased with thee *neka koti sahassani bhariya 'tthaya dayi mam* many thousands of *koti* times thou gavest me away as wife, etc., *neka koti sahassani upakar atthaya dayi mam*, many thousands of *koti* times thou gavest me away in order to obtain favour, etc.

Again it is said in the comment *agat agatanam yacakanam alankata patiyattam sisam kantilva gala lohitam niharitva anjitani kkhini uppatetva kula vansa padipikam putta manapa carinim bhariyamdenena namaya adinnamdanam nama nathi.* There is nothing that I refused to give away to those that came to me begging. I cut off my ornamented head, I sacrificed the blood of my neck, I plucked off my beautiful eyes, I gave away my promising children, and my beloved wife. The opponent's assertion was therefore palpable error or monstrous falsehood.

Mr. de Silva next pointed out the character of Bodhisat after he had the assurance of becoming Buddha. He was then *Buddhankura*, a germ of Buddahood growing up to attain that stage. A plant of any kind retained its nature when it grew.

In the *Parantapajataka* Bodhisat was heir apparent to the throne. Enemies having come to attack the city, the prince was asked by the king to drive them away. The prince, for fear of being killed, as was foretold by a she jackal, refused to go to battle. The king repeated his command, but

Bodhisat having for some time repeatedly refused to go, at last consented. But instead of protecting the city and the royal parent, he acted the part of an enemy. The royal parent, with the family priest and a servant called *Parantapa*, had to flee into the jungle for life. There the queen, Bodhisat's mother, fell in love with *Parantapa* and lived immorally with him, by whom the poor king was at last massacred; and in return the second prince, who was born in the jungle, when he grew up massacred *Parantapa* for seducing his mother the queen. All these things followed the treacherous conduct of Bodhisat, who acted the part of an enemy to his father, to his king, and to the kingdom. No civilised nation could countenance such misconduct and treachery.

In another birth, *Sussondiya Jataka*, Bodhisat was a gurula. He was a famous gambler. He went to Benares to gamble with the king Thambatanda and at last seduced the queen and ran away with her. This was the conduct of young Buddha.

In Matangajataka Bodhisat committed a similar act. Are these the examples set on record for those who would aspire to Buddhaship?

Now to inquire into Buddha's teachings.

In the *Satta Suriyuggana Suttani* of the Anguttara Nikaya, Buddha says:—

Sineru bhikkhave pabbata rájá caturasiti yojana sahassani ayamena caturasiti yojana sahassani vittharena caturasiti yojana sahassani maha samudde ajjhogalho caturasiti yojana sahassani maha samudáá accuggato.

Priests, the king of mountains is in length 84,000 yojanas, in breadth 84,000 yojanas, beneath the great ocean 84,000 yojanas and above the sea 84,000 yojanas. In the same suttam the order in which the world is destroyed is stated.

Hoti kho so bhikkhave samayo bahuni vassa satani bahuni vassa sahassani bahuni vassa sata sahassani devo na vassati; devo kho puna bhikkhave avassante ye keci bijagama bhutagama osadhi vana tina vanaspatayo te ussussanti vissussanti na bhavanti.

6

Priests, a time will come when for many hundreds, thou-sands, and hundred thousands of years there will be no rain. Priests, there being no rain, all plants, herbs, medicinal roots, forests, grass, and trees will become completely dried and burnt up. When the second sun appears, the little rivers, ponds, and lakes will become dried up and disappear. When the third sun appears, the large rivers, etc., will be dried up: when the fourth sun appears, the large lakes will be dried up. When the fifth sun appears, the seas will be dried up. When the sixth sun appears (*ayan ca maha pathari sineru ca pabbata raja adippanti pajjalanti*) this great earth and Mahameru will burn continually; thus this great earth and Mahameru, as well as everything else, are mentioned, and the order of their destruction. Where, then, is this great mountain which is 84,000 yojanas in length, 84,000 yojanas in breadth, and 84,000 yojanas above the sea, situated? How is it possible that it could not be seen to the eyes of men? this globe represents the earth. (Here the globe was shewn.) In this the shape of the earth, its dimensions, the great rivers and seas, and the positions of the countries, etc., are all represented. Now, the circumference of the earth is 25,000 miles. This is admitted by all the civilised nations of the world. This fact is proved by every day's experience. Therefore, a mountain with such dimensions could not exist on this earth. Wherever it existed it must be seen, as this globe which now stands on this little inkstand must be seen by all who are on the four sides of it. So likewise if there were a mountain of that kind it could not but be seen by all the inhabitants of the four quarters. Besides, man can know to a certainty within a few weeks whether there be such a mountain or not. Men at no period ever saw such a mountain, nor have they known by science that there could be such a mountain. One who had said that there was such a mountain cannot be supposed to have been a wise man, nor one who spoke the truth. That saying is a falsehood, it is an ignorant saying. It is moreover said that Sahampati made an offering of the size of Mahameru: that the re-sidence of Sakkraya was on the top of Mahameru, and that Buddha frequently went there; it is also said that Abhidharma was preached from its top. Many statements of this kind in connection with Mahameru are to be found scattered in the sacred books of Buddhism.

If it be asked why speak about Mahameru, the reply would be that if so great a falsehood could be uttered respecting a thing in this world, about which men can remove their doubts by seeing with their own eyes, how could any statement made touching heavenly and Brahma worlds, which we cannot see and examine, be believed? Is this person to be believed who speaks that which could easily be proved as false, and declares a thing not existing as if it existed? Certainly not. Besides, everything that is stated in Buddhism is connected with Mahameru.* The Chaturma-harajika, heavenly worlds, are connected with Mahameru. The Tawatinsa, heavenly world, is on the top of it. The other heavenly worlds gradually rise above it. The Brahma worlds are above those. The Arupa worlds are above the rest. Thus, if Mahameru did not exist where then could all those worlds exist? They must all tumble down, as a house whose foundation is rotten. Besides, if there is no Mahameru what advantage is there in almsgiving or perform-ing meritorious actions? They are done with a view to be born in those worlds. What is the use of observing Sil, precepts? They are observed to be born in the heavenly worlds. If those worlds do not exist all that is useless. What is the use of observing Jhána. abstruse meditations, as some priests at Matura observed until they got mad? All those things are useless. Mahameru, of 84,000 yojanas in length and breadth and height, must be placed on the earth;

---

* This reference on the part of the Rev. Mr. Silva to Meru (or Maha-meru)—termed in Hindu Mythology. " the navel of the earth,"—was, in our opinion. ill-timed and out of place in a discussion relating to Buddhism; and for the reason that it is Hinduism, rather than Buddhism. that has to do with *Meru*. This mountain, reputed so high and so broad, is traceable to Hindu legends, originating long before Buddha's time. The same mountain was referred to by Cleanthes and Anaximenes, shew-ing an interchange of thought between India and Greece. Buddhism bore something the same relation to Hinduism that Luther's Reformation bore to Roman Catholicism.

if not, Buddhism must be rejected at once. There is no advantage to be derived in believing in Buddhism.

Next, if Buddha had the power of knowing anything, even by meditation, it was proper for him to have given precepts, having in view how those precepts would be understood by his disciples; for because of the precept that his priests should not have carnal connection, one priest had connection with a female monkey, another priest with his own mother, and another with his own sister. How strange it is that one who professed to have the power of knowing everything should have given a precept which he ought to have foreseen would be misconstrued. Is there any other instance in the world where a teacher had brought up disciples in this way? Could not this omniscient one lay down the precept so as to prevent all these misunderstandings? If he had the power and did not use it, he was the cause of all these mischiefs. These are not the only instances mentioned in the Parajika book, but it contains a whole host of such filth.

Again, Buddha encouraged the practice of the most heinous crimes. A priest committed the foulest sin, the particulars of which cannot be given. The punishment Buddha inflicted upon the priest who so acted, was a *minor* punishment. The punishment was *thullacca*. He had simply to confess his fault before the priests, when he was retained in the priesthood. He was not even excommunicated.

Another priest was guilty of a horrible crime of the same kind. This crime was called by Buddha *dukkata*—very minor offence. The priest was retained in his priesthood, and associated with.

Another priest committed a similar offence: it was also called *dukkata*, a very minor offence.

Another instance of causing a miscarriage was pronounced *thullacca*; namely, the offence was very minute. Many other instances of this kind may be quoted from the *Parajika*. Were there instances of this kind recorded among the disciples of any other teacher? From the punishments given to such inhuman offenders, was it not clear that this teacher encouraged vice? Such offences would meet with the highest condemnation among men, but Buddha, by slighting, encouraged them. It is no use to say that the priests in Buddha's time were good men, because these instances shew the contrary.

With reference to Buddha's death, Buddha accepted the invitation of Chunda, the blacksmith. A young pig was prepared with rice. Buddha prevented the pork being served to any of his attending priests. He enjoyed it to satisfaction and it caused dysentery. The invitation was at Pawa. He had to go to Kusina from thence. Because of the dysentery, he suffered excruciating pains. He had to lie down twenty-five times on the way. He fainted several times. He called for water to quench his thirst. He managed to reach a little river, drank cold water, bathed in the river, but of this dysentery he never recovered. He died. These things are recorded in the Mahaparinibhana Suttan. His object in bringing these circumstances connected with his death was to shew that everything recorded about his birth, the gods and Brahmas attending on him, paying him glorious adorations, and Buddha's own miracles which he performed when required, were only statements which no one ought to credit. Here was the crisis in which all super-human attendance and comfort was necessary, and his own power needed to be manifested. Nothing of the kind was at hand. He got sick, he suffered pains, he walked from one place to another, fainting and lying down on the road, and at last died as any other miserable man would die. These things prove that the statements recorded about Buddha's super-human power were as fabulous as those related to lull children.

He then stated that, according to Christianity, man had an immortal soul as well as a body, which precious immortal soul must go from hence to the other world. In order to save this soul and take it to heaven, " God so loved the world that he gave his only begotten Son." This Jesus Christ, the Saviour of men, offered himself and died on the cross as a sacrifice for sin, by which a way is now opened to those who would be saved. He that believeth on him shall be saved. There is no other name given under heaven for man's salvation except this one name. Therefore it was the duty of all that were present to take refuge in that only Saviour and be saved from the miseries of hell. This he implored of all who were present to attend to.

Now, he said, no satisfactory answer was given to the objections brought forward against Buddhism, and every objection raised against Christianity was satisfactorily answered. This he begged the audience to bear in mind.

THE BUDDHIST'S CLOSING SPEECH,

OR

THE REV. MIGETTUWATTE'S FOURTH REPLY.

The Priest Migettuwatte, commencing his reply, said that this being the last hour of the controversy, it was the only opportunity he should have of addressing the assembly, and begged of them to listen to him patiently, and in as orderly a manner as during the previous occasions.

They would remember that the rev. gentleman on the first day of this controversy declared that Buddhism likened man unto beasts; in his morning lecture he most completely shewed that it was not Buddhism but Christianity that had done so; but as he now saw before him several who were not present on that occasion he would, to prevent any misconception, again read the passage appearing in the Bible in reference to this matter. It was Ecclesiastes iii. 19, and the words were, "For that which befalleth the sons of men befalleth beasts; even one thing befalleth them: as the one dieth, so dieth the other; so that a man hath no pre-eminence above a beast: for all is vanity." What clearer proof did they require to establish the fact that it was Christianity that likened man unto beasts and not Buddhism, as the rev. gentleman had improperly asserted.

With reference to his brief explanation of *Paticca-samuphada*, the rev. gentleman sneeringly asked whether he (the Priest) was more competent to understand this abstruse subject than Buddhaghosa, whose saying that one attempting to explain this doctrine was like a man who fell into the deep ocean he had cited. It was true that he had quoted this passage to illustrate the difficulty of properly comprehending this doctrine, but his explaining the subject to the utmost of his ability did not make him (the Priest) cleverer than Buddhaghosa. He could only attribute these stupid remarks touching his speech to the rev. gentleman's envious feeling towards him.

The rev. gentleman, in explaining *Paticcasamuphada,* uttered some arrant nonsense, and declared that this doctrine of causation was as confused and senseless as the statement that the father was begotten of the son, and the son was begotten of the father. This far-fetched illustration, he was sure, would not have been adduced by the rev. gentleman if he had the least idea of the correct meaning of *Paticca-samuphada.* He was in no manner justified in attributing to *Buddhism* the advocacy of such a circumlocutory genesis as his illustration implied. Buddhism did not contain any such doctrine, but it was in Christianity that mention was made of an extraordinary roundabout causation as instanced by the rev. gentleman.

He would crave their most careful attention while he partially explained what it was. As Mary, the Mother of Christ, was created by Jehovah, Jehovah was her father, and Mary his daughter; but because the Holy Ghost was conceived in Mary's womb Jehovah becomes her son, and Mary, Jehovah's mother; and as Christ is Jehovah's son, Jehovah becomes Mary's husband, and Mary his wife. So according to the Scriptures the same Mary becomes in one case Jehovah's daughter, in another Jehovah's mother, again Jehovah's wife, and truly if the term " roundabout " or " circumlocutory genesis " could be applied to any proceeding, it was to the Trinity notion connected with the birth of Christ, and not to the reasonable doctrine of *Paticcasamuphada.* He hoped that now they were satisfied that it was in Christianity and not in Buddhism that a father is said to be born of a son and son of a father.

The rev. gentleman also remarked, like his friend the Catechist, that the Buddhist doctrines could not be relied on as they were consigned to. writing about 450 years after Buddha's attaining *Nirvana*; in reply to this he need only repeat what he previously asserted, that there was abundant proof to shew that even during Buddha's lifetime, permanency was given to his doctrines in writing. And the Buddhist scriptures, he would assure them, did not share the same fate as a portion of the original Christian Bible, which was once completely burnt, but subsequently cooked up by a Kapua (devil's priest) of a temple and palmed off as a true copy of the original document.

The charge of murder raised by the rev. gentleman against Angulimala Terunanse was totally *untrue?* It never appeared in any Buddhist works that even an ant had been killed by him, much less a man. The name Angulimala was given to this personage after his ordination and the attainment of the Rahat state; and it was to this *Rahat* that offerings and oblations were made by Buddhists, and so even if Angulimala Thero were guilty of the alleged crime (which he was not, and which his opponent could not substantiate) while he was a layman, possessed of carnal desires and sinful passions, no blame attaches to him after his becoming a Rahat; and it could not be brought forward now as a slur on him, *after* he had attained that state, having made *full* expiation for all short-comings. The same remarks will apply to the rev. gentleman's strictures on Harantika and Alawaka as well.

The rev. gentleman sought to attach blame on the holy Rahats, Angulimala, Harantika, and Alawaka, who wrote the Buddhist scriptures, and said that the Bible, however, was pure, though written in part by the murderer Moses, who fled the country, and subsequently joined Jehovah. My opponent talked something about " filth " in Buddhist books. The charge is false and untrue! But if there were more filthy things in print than might be found in some parts of the Christian's Bible, he had not seen them.

The rev. gentleman can never prove from the Bible that Moses was free from sin even after he joined Jehovah. He was a man as are others, full of lustful desires and passions, and is even said to have slain thousands after this event. Surely they would not call such a man holy, and what credence can be placed on a work emanating from such a despicable source? But it was not

so with the writers of the Buddhist scriptures, who were all
Rahats, freed from all passions and lust, and whose sins had
been completely expiated And the attempt of the rev.
gentleman to asperse their holy character by mentioning
some of the shortcomings they may have been guilty of in a
previous state of existence, was as unsuccessful as disgraceful.
By such a course, Moses' crimes could not be extenuated;
and to hope to gain future happiness by believing in the
doctrines of such cruel and sinful men as Moses could only
be likened to an attempt to extract oil from sand !

To shew that Buddha gave away his wife to others,
the rev. gentleman read some Pali stanzas, and declared
them to be quotations from Buddhist scriptures. His
opponent knew better. Nothing of the sort could be
established from the stanzas quoted from the *Terapada-*
naya; and as for the other stanzas beginning *Ayatagala-*
nani such a passage as the rev. gentleman alleged never
appears amongst Buddha's sayings! He regretted much
for being under the necessity of having to argue in matters
of religion with one who did not hesitate to speak such
untruths, with the view of deceiving the ignorant. This,
however, would help those present to form a correct estimate
of the character of the rev. gentleman.

He also disparaged the character of Buddha by
quoting from *Parantapajataka* and *Sussandyajataka*; but
he would again tell them, as in the case of Angulimala,
that Holy Buddha was not to be blamed for sins committed in a previous birth, or even in a Bhodisat state,
which meant the state in which a being aspires to be a
Buddha. In both those states mortal beings are not devoid
of passions, but are liable to err. It was not correct to say
that Buddhists take refuge in such as these. Bhodisats are
neither worshipped nor resorted to for refuge, because they
do not pretend to possess the virtues of the Buddhas. The
interpretation given to *Budhankara* as being a growing
Buddha, is false and only shews the lamentable ignorance
of the rev. gentleman! So much for his unsuccessful
attempt to bring Buddha into contempt for offences committed in a Bhodisat state.

After shewing from *Surryotgamansatra* that Buddha had declared the existence of *Mahameru*, the rev. gentleman stated that even a schoolboy could satisfactorily disprove his statement. The rev gentleman no doubt alluded to Sir Isaac Newton's theory when he made that remark, according to which day and night were caused by the earth revolving round its axis, and not by the sun being hidden behind *Mahameru*. The little globe which the rev. gentleman produced was one made on Newton's principle: but even amongst Englishmen there were serious doubts and differences of opinion as to whether Newton's theory was correct or not. Among others, Mr. Morrison, a learned gentleman, had published a book refuting Newton's arguments, and he would be happy to allow the Christian party a sight of this book, which was in his possession. (Here he produced and handed around the "New Principia," by R. J. Morrison, F.A.S.L., published in London.)

How unjust, then, to attempt to demolish the great Buddha's sayings by quoting as authority an immature system of astronomy, the correctness of which is not yet accepted. Besides, even according to Christianity, the rev. gentleman's statements are incorrect. For in Ecclesiastes i. 5, appeared the words: "The sun also ariseth, and the sun goeth down, and hasteth to his place where he arose," which was biblically conclusive as to the sun moving, and the earth being stationary. There was a similar statement made in Buddhist books. The rev. gentleman's attempt to deny the existence of Mahameru with the aid of this little globe and Newton's theory, has only given the lie to his own religion.

The mariner's compass was the best proof he could give them of the existence of Mahameru. Keep it where you may, the attraction of the magnetic needle is always towards the North. This demonstrated that there was a huge mass in that direction which attracted the needle towards it, and according to the Buddhist books, Mahameru, the grandest and most stupendous rock on the face of the earth, was situated in the North. Were they not now satisfied that their Mahameru did exist in the North, as is declared? If not, can the Christian party adduce a single reason why there should be this attraction in the needle towards the North more than to the East, West, or South? This was impossible The mariner's compass was the mo t conclusive argument for the existence of the famed Mahameru. The passage through the northern zone of ice into the open Polar Sea, where are lands, rocks, and mountains, may demonstrate this beyond a doubt. * The rev. gentleman has asked how a rock 84,000 yojanas above the sea could exist on the earth, the circumference of which was only 25,000 miles. But this has been questioned as it is based on Newton's theory, and besides, it was not possible to draw any correct comparisons between the figures, because even at the present day the true length of a yodun is a controverted point among the *savants* in India. Has the rev. gentleman discovered the true measure? He would not argue further on the point, as he hoped that he had, to the complete satisfaction of the assembly, proved the existence of Mahameru, and demolished what the rev. gentleman had urged against its existence.

The rev. gentleman, amongst other matters brought against Buddhism, stated that a certain priest of Matara had gone mad by over-meditation; that was not strange, considering that meditation pure and simple, unaccompanied by philanthropic works and true piety, is said in Buddhist books to beget madness. Further, what had a man's madness or sickness to do with the truth or falsity of a religion?

The very mention of the horrible crimes for which punishments had been provided in the Vinaya, the Buddhist code of morals, demonstrated the purity of Bud-

---

* Some of the Buddhist priests are thoroughly versed in the works of modern scientists. Spending part of a day at the Widyodaga College of Buddhist professors and priests, near Colombo, Ceylon, and conversing with them upon the nature of soul, its attributes and its forces, Professor H. Sumangala. sending to his library, called my attention to a passage in Dr. Louis Buchner's work on "Matter and Force." Some of the books of Bishop Colenso have been translated into the Singhalese of Ceylon, by the Buddh sts,

dhism, since it shewed that remedies had been provided for every emergency. Of course, he (the Priest) was not to blame for declaring these heinous crimes before this assembly, the rev. gentleman was responsible for it, and his ignorance of what he was speaking about was more than once shewn in the interpretation he had given to some of the passages appearing in *Vinaya*. It did not, of course, appear that those priests who committed offences before the promulgation of these rules were punished with rigour, and what lawgiver would punish a man for an offence, though it may have been one *per se*, before the enactment of the ordinance? Let him assure them once for all that no blame could be attached to Buddhism, or any other religion, because of the immorality of some of its preachers. Who would dream of adducing the argument that Christianity was false because the wife of a well-known Protestant clergyman, when she got ill went awhile since to a distant village, and with the connivance of her husband, performed a *devil ceremony*, though he well knew of such an instance? Missionaries coming to this country have not always proved themselves either saintly or moral. How will the rev. gentleman get over the innumerable immoralities mentioned in the Bible for instance, that affair of Lot and his daughter, the incest committed by the sons and daughters of Eve, and a host of others?

The *pork* and the *rice* did not cause Buddha's death, as alleged by the rev. gentleman, but the incident was variously recorded to shew the nature of food partaken of by Buddha before his death. He would have died at the appointed day even if he had not tasted it. Buddha and Buddhist priests partake of what is put before them. They depend upon alms. They take neither scrip nor purse. They hold all life sacred. Some will not taste of animal food. And yet, after all, what was there so very unclean in pork? was it not better than the locusts made mention of in the Bible that were eaten by John the Baptist?

He had now to answer some objections raised by the Catechist in his speech, and he would do so briefly. His friend, the Catechist, had said that the taking refuge in Buddha, in the *Dhamma* or doctrines, and in the priesthood was all in vain, because in the first instance Buddha is dead and gone, and there could be no help from him; but if the Catechist understood what was written on this subject aright, he would not have uttered such astonishing folly. Buddha's death, it is recorded, consisted of three stages, the death of the passions, of the Skhandas, which he had previously explained, and of his relics. The death of his passions took place at the foot of the Bo-tree on his attaining Buddahood, that of the *Skhandas* was at the Sal-grove of King Mallava, and the last stage, that of the complete destruction of relics, is to take place 5,000 years after Buddha's attaining Nirvana, that is, about 2,500 years from the present time, when all Buddha's relics will be brought together near the Jayamaha Bo-tree in India, assume the form of a living Buddha, and after preaching for a short time will to the external cease to exist. Up to such time, the effect of Buddha's attaining Nirvana is not complete, and much merit can be gained by those who with faith make oblations and reverence these relics as Buddha himself. Buddha is yet connected with all that he ever touched, and all that he ever did on earth. Therefore to say that Buddha's influence does not exist at the present time is extremely false.

The *Sarana* in Buddhist *Dharma* did not mean taking refuge in Bana books, but in his doctrines, which if one believed aright, he would be saved in a future state; and that in the priesthood did not apply to sinful priests, but to those devoid of sin and passions.

As to the Upassampada controversy which the Catechist said was being carried on by the sects of Amerapura and Siam, he could assure them that not a single priest of any position of either party took any part in this controversy. It was simply a controversy carried on anonymously by two interested parties in the columns of *The Lakrivikirana*.

With reference to the charge that Buddha was not omniscient, and if he were that he ought to have known whether Alarakalama and others to whom he decided to preach, were alive or not, he (the Priest) said that this matter was brought forward at every controversy the Christians had with the Buddhists; and as it was on every occasion satisfactorily answered, his present explanation would be brief. It was true that Buddha was omniscient, but his omniscience was not of such an unpleasant nature as that ascribed to Jehovah, who it is declared sees and knows everything without directing his attention to it. What a filthy vista must be ever open to him, if without any effort of his, all the misery, filth, sin, uncleanness, and pollution of this world is continually seen by him! How could anyone be happy if compelled to witness all the misery and dirt of this earth? Did they not consider that Jehovah suffered more misery thus than in hell if, being in heaven, he necessarily witnessed all this? Buddha's omniscience was. however, far different ; he only discovered and saw what he wanted to by directing his power to it. True, from his past experience of Alarakalama and another, he determined upon preaching his doctrines to them as being men who were capable of understanding them; but as speedily as this determination was made a god intimated to him that those personages had died, and then it is said that he exercised his power of omniscience, and saw *even* the state in which Alarakalama had been born after death. He hoped the assembly now understood the pleasant and rational nature of Buddha's omniscience; and for the Christian party to say that he did not possess this power, simply because he did not exercise it, was like saying that a man who had full power of vision was blind because he did not turn his eyes to a certain object. So much for Buddha's omniscience.

Now a word touching Christianity. His (the Priest's) object in engaging in this controversy was simply the ascertainment of truth. He knew that Buddhism was true, and he had come to defend it ; but he was not so prejudiced in its favour as not to be open to conviction, and even to embrace Christianity, if they were able to prove it to be true; but what was there in it to be believed?

Why should the Christians lay so much stress on the death of Christ, who had been killed by the authorities for attempting to rise in rebellion against the Roman Empire? What else could the "powers" do to a man who had openly advised his followers to sell even their clothes and provide themselves with swords! and whose crime, according to the inscription placed on the cross, was that of styling himself the King of the Jews!—a nation then under the Roman Empire.

Besides, how unsatisfactory was the evidence · as to his bodily resurrection. The first witness they had to testify to this all-important event, according to Mark xvi. 9, was Mary Magdalene, who, they would remember, was a woman who had at one time been possessed of seven devils! What weight could be attached to the evidence of such a mad woman? The fact was that Christ's body was removed from the tomb by his disciples on the night when there were no guards, and how significant were the words in the Scriptures that even at that time it was rumoured that his body had been "stolen" away? Well, if they were satisfied with this resurrection of Christ, they should believe it by all means!

The Christians declare that God's spirit will be with those who believe on him. He (the Priest) did not deny belief in a Creator, but admitted that he owed his existence to one; but why should man be allowed to become the enemy of the Creator which, according to the Bible, he now was? The Christians' theory of a Creator was false, and he would presently explain to them who the true Creator was, in whom he believed, and what he had to say would be borne out even by the Scripture account of the creation. He must say that this part of the Bible was most prudently written by one who was in no way ignorant. It was there said that the spirit of God moved upon the face of the waters, and why should this fact have been mentioned if not to shew that the acting of this spirit on the water was the cause of all animal and vegetable life? This was certainly so. The action of air on water always produced animal life; if a cocoanut, which usually remains on the tree without rotting for nine or ten months, be pierced through and air be allowed to enter into it, the water inside was sure to breed worms; and so long as air could be excluded from water, there was no generation of any insect. Likewise in this instance, "the spirit of God," as it was called, acted upon the face of the waters, and it produced animal life.

The origin of all species was then, even according to the Bible, "breath," or air, with which was associated heat and water. To these three, air, heat, and water, by whatever name known, whether Brahma, Vishnu, and Iswara, or God, Son, and Holy Ghost, were attributable the origin of species. These, so far as would be comprehended, were their only creator; and him he would reverence; and as neither air, nor water, nor heat could produce alone without the aid of the other, but were co-existent, and so closely associated with each other that they could not be said to have separate existences, the Christians were justified in saying that though there are three beings, the Father, Son, and Holy Ghost, yet they were not three Gods, but one God. These, however, were not beings, but states. There is one Absolute Spirit in and over all.

It was also declared in the Bible that Satan tempted Adam and Eve to eat of the forbidden fruit. Here he was certain that "Satan" meant lust, and "eating the forbidden fruit" signified carnal knowledge, which produced child-birth and all the other baneful consequences mentioned in the Bible. "Eating the forbidden fruit" could mean nothing else, for if sorrow in child-bearing was the punishment for actually eating the fruit, in the literal sense of the words, how could they account for the agony that many members of the brute creation suffer when giving birth to their young? For instance, the travail the *Polongas* suffer is so great that they sometimes burst whilst giving birth to their young. Had they also eaten of the forbidden fruit? Such was Christianity! It was full of irrational and unreasonable notions.

But as for Buddhism, the most eminent had in all ages given their testimony in favour of it. The great doctors of the science of medicine, of the efficacy of which there can be only one opinion, the originators of ethics, the propounders of that important and wonderful science, astrology, by which even the date of the death of a man could be accurately foretold, not to mention details, and the names of learned men, always invoked the aid of Buddha and extolled the praises of him and of his religion, in every one of their works.

Buddhism inculcated the purest morality and urged the necessity of self-denial, self-sacrifice, and charity. It encouraged peace. It tolerated all religions in its midst. It had nothing to fear. It pleaded of men to follow the example of Holy Buddha, and pointed the sick and the sorrowing to the blissful state of Nirvana. Quantities of books could be adduced in proof of these teachings, but it was needless to so do, as he had, he hoped, to the complete satisfaction of his auditory, proved the truth of Buddhism and the falsity of Christianity. He also trusted that they had not forgotten the nature of the answers adduced by the opposite side, to meet the objections raised by him; and lastly, he would now earnestly beg of them to bear these things in mind, and always take refuge in Holy Buddha.

Scarcely had the last words of the above lecture been uttered, when cries of " Sadu " ascended from the thousands who were present. Endeavours were made by the handful of police to keep order, but nothing induced them to cease their vociferous cries until, at the request of the learned High Priest of Adam's Peak, the Priest Migettuwatte again rose, and with a wave of his hand, beckoned to the men to be quiet, when all was still."

REMARKS.

Thus ends a very spirited discussion, in which a Buddhist priest—called a " heathen,"—appealing to various Bibles, to reason, and to the common sense of the gathered thousands, bravely met a Christian minister in a square face-to-face controversy. The reading deeply interested me; the more so, perhaps, from perusing it in Ceylon, near the spot where it transpired. The only thing that seriously mars the flow of thought while turning over the pages is the bitterness, and even offensive personalities, occasionally indulged in by the otherwise eloquent disputants. Even if the Christians—as I was credibly informed—were the aggressive party in commencing the caustic, brow-beating style of argument, the Buddhist Priest was hardly justifiable in following the example. It was a bad one. Peace, calmness, and contemplation constitute practically the very genius of Buddhism. And in all religions it is the better way to return good for evil, and kind for bitter words. The Quaker poet of America wrote these telling lines :—

"The truth's worst foe is he who claims
   To act as God's avenger,
And dreams, beyond his sentry beat,
   The crystal walls in danger.

Who sets for heresy his traps
   Of verbal quirk and quibble,
And weeds the garden of the Lord
   With Satan's borrowed dibble."

Both Gautama Buddha and Jesus not only taught, or laid down, the principle of returning blessing for cursing, but they beautifully exemplified their teachings in lives of tenderest charity and forgiveness.

"Before and during the Vedic era," writes the scholarly Sir M. Coomara Swamy, "it was the shedding of blood, the sacrifice of man or beast, the oblations of butter and milk, the worship of fire and the warring of elements, which marked the awakening of the supernatural sentiment in the Hindu breast. But anon a change came over the land. Peace, gentleness, and all the mild virtues gained the ascendant. True sacrifice, it was taught, was self-sacrifice. The preparation for heaven consisted in the destruction of all evil passions. And the greatest happiness, it was inculcated, consisted in a life of philosophic trust and quiet."

As a sample of Gautama Buddha's sermonising, I select the following from the Khappavisána Sutta, and the commentaries. The discourse was delivered by this Indian sage, so it seems, at the request of Ananda, a disciple of considerable distinction.

"Seek first for the true path, and when finding, diligently follow in it. The true hero, abandoning the vanity of life, and fors___ing the foolish ways of the world, flings off the bands of the household like a kovilara tree its leaves, and walks alone. He who has houses, and fields, and cattle, and children grieves; but he who is content, who has no object of selfish desires, does not grieve. The greatest is he who, desiring the least, gives the most. Humility is better than honour. . . . I learned a lesson from one who sat calm and happy by the way-side, asking alms of the rich that he might bestow them upon the poor. . . . The Brahmans, protected by virtue, were not 'injured by others. They were invincible. None ever stopped them at the doors of their houses. Formerly they practised celibacy from their youth up to their forty-eighth year. The more consecrated continued pure unto the end of life. He who frees himself from lasciviousness, refuses to recount worthless stories, abandons inordinate laughter, and yields not to greediness, worldliness, and hypocrisy, becomes established in peace, and knows what constitutes the true essence of wisdom and peacefulness. . . . Good friends may be admitted into one's company; but not obtaining such friends, let one subsist upon pure food, engage in prayer, and walk alone. . . . I lived for a night on the banks of the Mahi; the house was roofless, the fire was extinguished by the rain, and yet I was happy, because free from anger, free from stubbornness, free from passions." "Like an ox that has broken its bindings, like an elephant that has broken the galucchi creeper, I have broken the chain of worldly attachment. I shall not return for re-birth. I shall enter Nirvana." . . . "My mind is free from passions, is released from the follies of the world, has long been under training, is under thorough control; there is no sin whatever in me. I have obtained the victory."

Thus spake Buddha to Ananda, and other disciples.

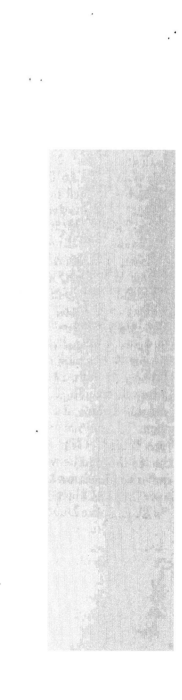

Modern Spiritualism.

By EPES SARGENT.

PLANCHETTE : THE DESPAIR OF SCIENCE.

Being a Full Account of Modern Spiritualism.

Price, in Illuminated Paper Covers, $1; in Green Cloth, $1.25. Postage, 16c.
A New Edition, just issued by Roberts Brothers, Boston.

This volume should be properly called " A History of Modern Spir Itualism," for it is a thorough and careful survey of the whole subject of well-attested phenomena believed to be spiritual.

Prof. WM. CROOKES, F. R. S., of London, the celebrated chemist, whose scientific verifications of the spiritual phenomena are now creating such a sensation, writes, under date of April 17, 1874, —
"*Planchette* was the first book I read on Spiritualism, and it still remains in my opinion, the best work to place in the hands of the uninitiated."

GEO. WM. CURTIS, in HARPER'S WEEKLY, says of it, —
"It is a copious and popular but faithful summary of the phenomena and theories. The ample knowledge and literary skill with which the subject is treated make this volume an indispensable manual to all who are attracted to this speculation, and it will be read with great interest by the skeptic as well as by the believer."

The Rev. Dr. BELLOWS, in the LIBERAL CHRISTIAN, says of it, —
"It sets forth many important considerations with regard to the philosophy of the mind, while its historical notices of the development of Spiritualism during the last twenty years give a more complete and impartial view of the phenomena in question than has thus far been presented to the public."

The New York Express says, —
"This is certainly one of the most startling works of our sensational age. It purports to give a duly authenticated narration of spiritual manifestations, which are beyond the bounds of credulity by any calm think ing reader; and yet the asserted facts are given with such an apparent truthfulness and distinctness of detail, and the learned and distinguished names connected with the scenes described are of such weight, that it is impossible to deny the conviction impressed upon the mind that either Spiritualism is one of the greatest delusions of the age, or that it is indeed a new manifestation of supernatural power, deserving the investigations of our theologians and teachers. The work, from its extreme interest, will amply repay a careful perusal."

The Boston Journal says, —
"Mr. Sargent has here collected a vast amount of information, and whoever wishes to have an intelligent epitome of the whole history of modern Spiritualism will find it in this volume."

For Sale by

COLBY AND RICH,

No. 9 Montgomery Place, Boston, Mass.

A BIOGRAPHY

OF

MRS. J. H. CONANT,

The World's Medium of the Nineteenth
Century.

A HISTORY OF HER MEDIUMSHIP

From Childhood to the Present Time;

BEING A NARRATIVE OF THE

Personal Experiences, Sharp Trials, and Liberalizing
Victories achieved in the cause of Human
Reason and Spiritual Knowledge.

Let the heart-stricken read it, and be comforted;
Let the earth-weary peruse it, and be glad;
Let the world's workers explore it, and be encouraged;
Let the doubter scan its incontrovertible testimony, and be confounded;
Let the true man and woman, wherever abiding, recognize in it the
life-line of a *kindred soul.*

COLBY AND RICH,

PUBLISHERS,

NO. 9 MONTGOMERY PLACE,

BOSTON, MASS.

FLASHES OF LIGHT

FROM

THE SPIRIT-LAND,

THROUGH THE MEDIUMSHIP OF

MRS. J. H. CONANT.

COMPILED AND ARRANGED BY

ALLEN PUTNAM,

Author of "Spirit-Works;" "Natty, a Spirit;" "Mesmerism, Spiritualism,
Witchcraft, and Miracle;" Etc., Etc.

This comprehensive volume of more than four hundred pages
will present to the reader a wide range of useful information
upon subjects of the utmost importance.

THE DISEMBODIED MINDS

of many distinguished lights of the past

HERE SPEAK

to the embodied intelligences of to-day, proclaiming their views
as derived from or modified by the FREEDOM FROM ARTIFICIAL
CONSTRAINT, and the ADDED LIGHT OF THE SPIRIT-
WORLD, concerning

THE ORIGIN OF MAN,

the duty devolving upon each individual, and the

DESTINY OF THE RACE.

As an Encyclopædia of Spiritual Information, this work is
without a superior.

Price $1.50.   Postage 22 cents.

COLBY AND RICH, PUBLISHERS,

9 Montgomery Place, Boston.

Milton Keynes UK
Ingram Content Group UK Ltd.
UKHW030620141024
2164UKWH00010B/63